Seven Rules of Retirement Investment

Principles to Build and Maintain Personal Wealth

By: David M. Rogers, President, Life Equation Institute

Introduction

1) Rule 1 – Pay Yourself First.

- Lifestyles Often Grow to Equal or Exceed Income
- Financial Discipline Equates to Living Within Your Means
- Always Set Aside Money for Yourself First
- Identify Vehicles that Force You to Pay Yourself First

2) Rule 2 – Starting Earlier is More Effective than Starting Later.

- You Can begin as Early as Age Twenty One to Use Tax-Deferred Vehicles
- The Later You Start, the More You Must Pay Yourself
- Compound Growth Equals Financial Power; the Advantage of Interest and Time
- Two Case Examples of an Early and Late Saver

3) Rule 3 – Always Have a Plan.

- A Plan Establishes Goals and Direction
- Envision Your Retirement Lifestyle and Replacement Income
- Finding Your Magic Number
- Use Any and All available Professional Resources
- Your Own Research and Education is Critical
- Periodically Review and Make Adjustments to Your Plan
- Your Strategies Should Reflect Your Plans and Intentions
- Sample Financial Plan for a Working Professional
- A Few Financial Concepts to Study

4 – Tax-Deferred Investments Grow Faster than Similar Taxable Investments.

Capital Gains, Dividend and Interest Income Taxes Reduce Your Investment's Net Growth
Tax-Deferred Vehicles May Include Employer added Benefits
Tax-Deferred Vehicles Provide Incentives to Remain Invested.
The Tax Game: Assumptions about Present and Future Tax Brackets

Introduction

One of the most serious concerns facing Americans today is the strategic financial planning that will allow for the average employee to retire comfortably after an ordinary thirty-five to forty year career. For many, the central object of the American dream is financial success and the achievement of financial independence at some point along the timeline of productive working years. The pathway to a comfortable retirement is undoubtedly in the thoughts of every working American at some point or another in their working lives. What everyone who picks up this book should realize is that you are a potential millionaire in the making upon retirement. It does not matter what you do, how much you earn or where your working life may take you. If you plan far enough ahead, you can retire comfortably. While we have an entire financial services industry anxious to help a working individual plan for and solve the investment issues of retirement planning, it is helpful to initially understand the basic principles necessary to build toward the day when full-time employment is no longer a necessity of life. Seven Rules for Retirement Investment outlines the fundamental principles that each of us should internalize and consider in forming our own personal road map to financial comfort and independence. Each rule covers a specific principle that will allow you, the reader, to form a framework that will better equip you to sort through and select from the myriad of products, ideas and details that will be faced in making and executing a plan for an enjoyable retirement. These principles will arm you with a fundamental understanding of the whys of retirement planning to assist in making better use of the specifics of what and when in retirement planning.

The traditional paths to replacement of working income during the retirement years have changed under an ever shifting environment of financial crisis and competition. The traditional pension plans that were the cornerstone of many organizations' retirement strategies for their employees become rarer each passing year. Many of these types of retirement plans that still do exist provide benefit levels that are far below any amount needed for a reasonable lifestyle upon retirement. The foundations of our Social Security system are threatened with extinction. Both financial mismanagement and a shrinking worker to retiree ratio are squeezing the system to death. There are many working Americans who currently pay into the system who are wondering if there will indeed be any funds available when it is their turn to receive benefits in the coming years. In essence, the responsibility for income replacement in the retirement years has been steadily shifted from the employer and government to the individual. If the average working American does not recognize and respond to these changes, they will find themselves a day late and a dollar short when the golden years inevitably arrive.

Fortunately, there are numerous vehicles available under the current tax code that will allow you, the working, taxpaying individual, to plan and provide for yourself. That is, if you understand the basic principles found in this book and use them as soon as you gain an understanding and are able to apply them. Time is always on your side if you plan far enough ahead. But whatever you do, start today to formulate and execute a plan. Your future depends upon it. If you already have a basic plan in place, evaluate that plan in light of the principles put forth in this book. The more that you know, the more effective you can be in managing your personal pathway to retirement. Whatever your situation, there is a way to plan, execute and succeed at securing your own financial future. Financial freedom is personal freedom. They go hand in hand. So let's explore the fundamental principles that can literally set you free from future financial worries and provide the privileges you have always dreamed of at a time in life when they will be most appreciated.

Rule 1 – Pay Yourself First

The fact is that retirement planning should be given careful consideration from the day you embark upon a career. We work for many reasons. No matter how strong our desire to fulfill our own abilities, contribute to society, embark upon a working adventure or change the world for the better, financial realities have to be part of the equation. The average career training involves the details and tools necessary to be proficient at a specific job or set of tasks. Managing your retirement requires attention to detail and specific tasks also. These tasks and details will need to be repeated many times over the course of your working career. It is not just *how* you execute these details, but *why* you must execute them frequently and correctly to be successful in your overall goal. And that goal should always be to have the financial resources available, once you reach an age or point in life where a full-time, wage earning job comes to an end, to maintain your desired lifestyle.

The first and overriding principle of retirement planning is simply this – you can ultimately rely on nothing or no one else to provide for retirement savings more than you must rely upon yourself. It is your responsibility to take charge of this aspect of your financial life, plain and simple. The responsibility for your retirement planning cannot be subrogated to your employer, union or to the government. Once you come face to face with this responsibility and accept it, you have started on the pathway toward planning and performance. Once you have understood that something must be done, and you are the one who has to do it, you are prepared to immerse yourself in the details. Once you fully take responsibility for yourself, the first rule you must be disciplined to follow is to *pay yourself first*. It is not that complicated to pay yourself first. As this chapter will explore, there are all sorts of methods and vehicles that will allow you to do it. You simply have to take the time to go and make it happen.

Lifestyles Often Grow to Equal or Exceed Income

You will spend the entirety of your working career earning and spending. The standard expenses of life are ever present – food, housing, clothing, transportation, health care, education, etc. If there is one observable fact that describes personal financial management in the modern world it is this: whatever your net income, you will eventually discover a lifestyle that requires the complete expenditure of that income. In other words, you will spend what you earn. There may be exceptions to this rule when personal earnings may greatly exceed the norm. However, a trail of broken athletes and celebrities who at one time earned millions, even tens of millions of dollars, suggests planning and discipline are required at any level of income.

Even as your career skills and abilities increase, and correspondingly your income, financial demands and obstacles will almost certainly be encountered. Traditional family life and children seem to be as much a financial decision as a social decision or personal preference in modern life. What were once deemed luxuries are often seen as necessities in a modern middle-class household. As technology increases, so does the perceived need to posses and utilize new technologies, all of which comes at a cost. In a modern era of marketing, and within an economic framework that requires and encourages constant spending, the number of ways you can be parted from your earnings will constantly increase. There are many consumer goods that have yet to be invented that are statistically certain to attract your consumer dollar in the near future. You have to pay yourself first before all of the necessities, as well as the attractive spending opportunities, consume whatever income you may have available.

<u>Financial Discipline Equates to Living Within Your Means</u>

If you follow the trend of spending most or all that you earn, and statistically you already have or will fall into this category, you need to take steps immediately to pay yourself first. Once your earnings are spent, they are spent. A greater number of consumer goods will not see you through your retirement years, only retirement savings will support you. It requires financial discipline to pay yourself first and then determine to live on what is left. The fact is that it really does not require setting aside significant amounts of your income if your investment horizon is long enough. If you learn to pay yourself first, you will likely never miss the money you have earmarked for your retirement savings.

If you begin early enough in your working career, you may begin to build significant savings for retirement by setting aside between three and six percent of your gross wages. While this may seem significant to some, particularly if you are just starting out in a career and are at entry level pay scales, chances are you are able to discipline yourself to live on the remaining earnings after retirement savings deductions. Setting aside pre-tax earnings for retirement also reduces your tax burden, so you may not miss the funds as much as you might imagine. The later you begin however, the larger the amount you must set aside each month becomes. Such a late starting scenario may indeed infringe upon lifestyle choices

In the context of a broader discussion, financial discipline and living within your means are keys to lifelong financial success. Over the last generation, savings rates have declined sharply in the United States compared to other developed countries. Consumer debt has been relatively easy to secure and the trend to go into debt for depreciating and expendable consumer goods such as cars, furniture and electronics seems to be taxing our cumulative savings ability. The average American household carries more debt now than at any point in history. The trend is even institutionalized nationally as our own government is borrowing roughly thirty cents on every dollar they spend. Debt is not the friend of savings. Money spent to service debt on unnecessary luxuries is money that is not being utilized to pay yourself first. Only with constant self discipline in savings and spending can you be assured that you will pay yourself first. The chart below shows the declining trend in household savings over the last few decades in the United States. This is a trend that must be reversed if we are to maintain a healthy economy, much less plan and provide for our own retirement.

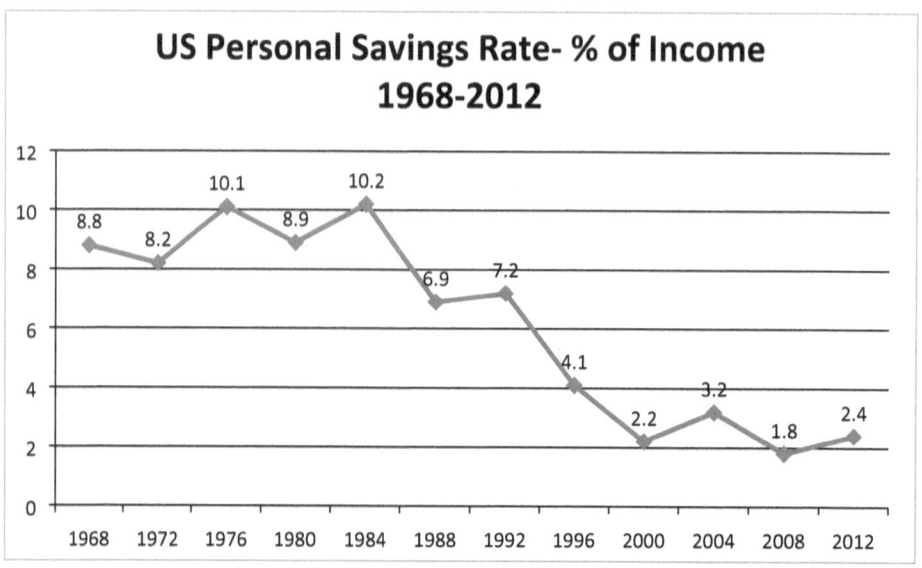

US Personal Savings Rate- % of Income
1968-2012

We live in an era where the economic necessity of spending all that we can is not only commonplace, it is encouraged. The last few decades have been the epitome of consumerism. Advertising media flourishes in numerous iterations that did not even exist a few years ago. Everywhere you turn you are encouraged to spend and buy, buy more and spend more. It is trendy to have the latest and greatest. There is very little incentive in the framework of modern consumerism that encourages you to save and plan. We live in a generation of instant gratification. We want it all and we want it now. As a result, consumer spending and average household debt continues to rise. Only the recent severe recession and the threat of national and global depression have resulted in a shift in thinking toward more conservative spending. While a complete discussion of needs versus wants exceeds the scope of the principle, it is nonetheless important to note. Discretionary spending should be examined regularly. Reasons for spending all of your earnings and not saving need to be seriously considered and rethought. A wide range of situational, habitual or behavioral factors should be carefully examined and put into context with the greater need to establish savings that you will retain long-term. Wisdom exists not in the fact that it is right or wrong to spend what is being earned, but in the reasons why a portion of your income is or is not being dedicated to building a brighter future. There are few legitimate reasons not to pay yourself first. The chart below illustrates the trend of total debt service as a percentage of household income. The higher your debt ratios obviously the less you have to save. The most disturbing trend has been in the last few decades where debt payments have actually exceeded household income. This trend obviously has catastrophic results and is not sustainable for any significant period of time.

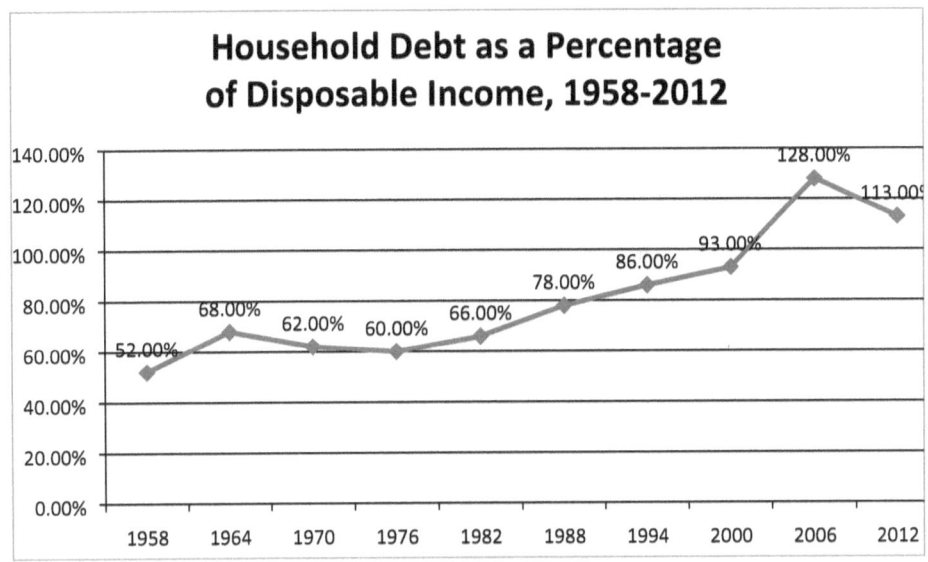

Household Debt as a Percentage of Disposable Income, 1958-2012

Data points shown: 52.00%, 68.00%, 62.00%, 60.00%, 66.00%, 78.00%, 86.00%, 93.00%, 128.00%, 113.00%

Years (x-axis): 1958, 1964, 1970, 1976, 1982, 1988, 1994, 2000, 2006, 2012

Y-axis: 0.00%, 20.00%, 40.00%, 60.00%, 80.00%, 100.00%, 120.00%, 140.00%

Identify Vehicles that Allow You to Pay Yourself First

No matter what your situation, no matter how great or how meager your earnings, there are ways that you can strategically pay yourself first. The current tax code allows for numerous financial vehicles that will allow you to set aside a certain amount of your earnings for retirement savings that are deducted from your gross pay. In most cases, these vehicles will funnel a percentage of your earnings into a retirement savings plan even before your earnings are distributed in a regular paycheck. There really is no excuse not to pay yourself first. The financial vehicles exist and it is a simple decision on your part to understand and utilize them.

Most retirement savings vehicles have specific financial advantages and restrictions in common. Most vehicles allow your investment income to grow on a tax deferred basis. The power of this advantage will be discussed more thoroughly in Rule 4. Also, most retirement savings vehicles provide incentives to keep your money in savings by imposing penalties if you try to access the monies before a certain age, usually incurring penalties if funds are withdrawn prior to age 59½. However, many plans have loan provisions that will allow you to borrow money from your plan at any time to pay certain life expenses, such as college tuition, as long as you repay the funds to your plan over a specified period of time. All vehicles require you to start taking a certain portion of the monies out as a distribution by a certain age, usually 70½. And most retirement vehicles will reduce your earned income by the amount put into savings on an annual basis. Most vehicles will allow for a wide variety of investment choices, although your investment options may be limited by who sponsors and/or administers a particular retirement savings plan.

Let's take a look at the most common retirement savings vehicles and review a few of the features that make them attractive:

Self-funded Traditional Investment Retirement Arrangements (IRA)

Personal Investment Retirement Arrangements, or Investment Retirement Accounts or IRAs as they are commonly known, are available to anyone over the age of twenty-one. An IRA is simply a savings account that you can open and contribute to in regular amounts that has designated tax-deferred status. In most cases, you must contribute to the account with money from your earnings after they are received. However, at the end of the tax year, your IRA contributions are deducted from your gross taxable income. IRAs, like most retirement vehicles have the distinct advantage of allowing your investment earnings to accrue on a tax-deferred basis. This means that you incur no tax liability on the earnings over the life of your IRA until you begin to take distributions. Then at that time, all monies coming out of the IRA are taxed as ordinary income at the then current tax rate. This has distinct advantages in earnings power over the life of your investments.

IRAs can be opened and invested in almost any type of financial tools you can imagine. Any bank, credit union, investment company or stock broker will have a multitude of options that can house your IRA savings and earn a return. There are also a number of companies that will allow you to self-direct your IRA savings into less traditional investments such as land, commodities or commercial real estate. Further, IRAs have the advantage of allowing other members of your extended family to make an IRA contribution on your behalf. The downside to traditional IRAs is that the contribution limits are fairly low. The maximum amount you can place in an IRA in 2013 is $5,500 per year if you are under the age of 50 and $6,500 per year if you are over 50. While this may seem like a comfortable amount, it is small in comparison to employer sponsored plans such as 401K or 457 plans. However, if you start early enough, it is still possible to amass significant savings into an IRA.

Also, there are offsets based on your access to employer sponsored plans and your annual gross income that can theoretically reduce your eligible contribution rate all the way to zero. In the practical world, IRAs are a vehicle available to those who may not have another primary source of retirement savings. They may also supplement to a small degree other retirement savings plans that are sponsored by an employer.

Roth IRAs

Roth IRAs are subject to the same deferral rules as traditional IRAs. The main difference is that funds you put into a Roth IRA are not deducted from your annual gross income. In essence, you are funding a Roth IRA with after tax dollars. The Roth IRA shares the same advantage as the traditional IRA in that all investment income in the IRA accrues without a tax liability year to year. Unlike the traditional IRA, the Roth IRA does not tax distributions once you begin taking them upon retirement. All future distributions from a Roth IRA are tax free and incur no liability in the years funds are distributed (as long as they are distributed after a certain age as defined by the tax code). While Roth IRAs do not enjoy the advantage of reducing your tax liability in the years you defer monies into them, they make up for this disadvantage by allowing tax free distributions of your investment earnings down the road. This is particularly effective if you are unsure about future tax rates and wish to minimize future tax liabilities. Roth IRAs are a powerful vehicle for retirement savings if you can assume a significant investment window with an opportunity to accrue substantial investment earnings over time.

Section 401K Plans

Section 401K plans are employer sponsored vehicles that allow larger amounts to be deferred than IRAs. If you work for or are looking to work for a company that sponsors a 401K plan or are a business owner, you may take advantage of the many benefits of participating in a 401K Plan once you meet the eligibility requirements of that plan. Eligibility for participation in this type of plan is usually achieved after a pre-determined period of time working for a particular employer full-time. In most cases you have to be employed for a minimum of six months to one year and be over the age of twenty-one to begin participation. Employers are required to have a description of all relevant aspects of such a plan on hand that you may freely access, called a Summary Plan Description. Many larger companies will also have in-house benefits experts that can walk you through the details and requirements necessary to take part in the plan. 401K plan provisions, including incentives given through matching employer funds, should always be considered as part of the overall compensation package a company has to offer. Salaries, bonuses, working conditions and other considerations should be weighed carefully in determining the attractiveness and viability of an employer. Benefits plans, particularly the possibilities a retirement savings plan brings, should be given careful thought also.

Section 401K of the tax code was enacted in 1978. It has developed over the years into a powerful and flexible vehicle for employers to provide incentives for employees to save a substantial amount of their earnings toward retirement. For the calendar year 2013, the deferral limits for 401K plans are $17,500, considerably more than an IRA. These deferral limits tend to rise year to year to keep pace with inflation. Additionally, depending on your income, you may be eligible to defer money into an IRA also, combining the savings power of both plans. If you are over the age of fifty, catch up provisions allow you to defer an additional $5,000 for a total of $22,500 into a 401K plan. These are effective deferral amounts based on income averages across the country. This type of plan is a primary way you can take responsibility to pay yourself first. 401K deferrals go into a professionally managed investment account where they grow over time to build a financially sound future.

Another advantage of employer sponsored 401Kplans is the potential of an employer match to employee deferred funds. According to the Profit Sharing/ 401K Council of America, an industry trade group, about 78% of 401K plans includes some kind of employer match for employee contributions. Employer matches have the capability of providing an immediate and substantial return on investment. Employer matches vary from plan to plan as there is no industry standard. Employer matches serve as a financial incentive for you to remain employed for more than a short period of time. They also serve as a prompt for employees to defer at least a certain percentage of their pay into qualified retirement savings plans. Let's look at some examples of employer matching provisions and what they infer about their respective retirement savings philosophies:

Example 1 – ABC Company has a 401K plan for all employees, hourly and salaried. Their plan will match employee deferrals dollar for dollar up to 3% of gross annual pay. This means if you earn $50,000 annually and elect to contribute 3% of your pay into the plan, you will defer $1,500 over the course of a year and the company will match your contributions with an additional $1,500. If you choose to defer 5% of your pay, you will contribute a total of $2,500 for the year but the match still tops out at $1,500, based on matching up to 3%. In this example, the employer is encouraging a minimal level of employee retirement savings and is incenting a 3% baseline for deferrals by providing an attractive match up to that pre-determined level.

Example 2 – XYZ Corporation has a retirement savings plan that matches employee contributions at $.50 for each dollar deferred up to 6% of gross pay. This means if you earn $50,000 annually and elect to contribute a full 6% of your pay into the plan, you will defer $3,000 over the course of a year and the company will match your contributions with an additional $1,500. In this example, the company is again suggesting a particular deferral target for their employees. By incenting up to 6% of pay, although not providing as generous a match percentage wise as in the first example, the company makes it attractive to defer at least that amount.

Example 3 – Company DEF sponsors a plan that matches $.50 on the dollar up to 6% of gross pay and $.25 on the dollar from 6% to 9% of gross pay. If you earned $50,000 and deferred the full 9%, you would defer a total of $4,500 in pay and earn a total of $1,875 in employer matching funds. In this example the company is incenting a minimum contribution of 6%, but offering additional reward for those employees who will exercise discipline in reaching a 9% deferral level. While the additional match is not as attractive as the lower 6%, it still provides a reward for those who will take a more aggressive approach to their retirement planning.

In addition to employer matches, companies can do discretionary profit sharing distributions into 401K plans. These distributions can be based on the company's profitability in a given year and must be distributed evenly to all plan participants based on their level of personal participation. For example, Company XYZ above might declare a profit sharing bonus in their 401K plan of an additional 4% of gross pay for all plan participants and your salary was $50,000, your portion of the additional employer profit sharing contribution would total $2,000.

The above examples illustrate the power of the 401K vehicle. If you worked for XYZ Company in the above examples, you would have deferred a total of 6% of your own money, or $3,000. Your immediate return on investment, however, is substantial. Your employer would have matched your deferral with $1,500 of matching contributions as well as $2,000 of profit sharing distributions. Before your retirement savings has earned a dime in investment income for you, you have already realized a return on investment for that year of 117% ($3,500/$3,000). Additionally you saved $750 in income tax that year, assuming you are taxed in a 25% tax bracket, on the $3,000 you deferred. Your investment income on those funds further enhances your return. All of this adds up to a powerful savings tool with attractive incentives.

Employer matches and profit sharing contributions in 401K plans are almost always subject to some sort of vesting provisions. Your own deferrals are always 100% vested. This means that the funds belong completely to you the moment they are put into the plan. If you were to leave that employer for another opportunity, your deferred funds would travel with you, or "rollover", into another sponsored plan or an IRA. Employer funds, however, are a different story. Because employers wish to encourage and incent loyalty, longevity and productivity out of their employees, matching employer funds and profit sharing contributions are subject to vesting requirements. This means that you must remain in their employment for a specific period of time before all of the matching funds accruing in your plan are eligible to travel with you if you should leave. Vesting provisions vary from company to company and from plan to plan. Regulations dictate that vesting provisions can be as liberal as a company wants them to be to provide incentive to their employees, but in no case can their vesting exceed the guidelines illustrated below. These illustrations are the maximum vesting schedules allowable for the two types of vesting provisions provided: graduated vesting and cliff vesting. Graduated vesting secures the employer funds over time, while cliff vesting allows the funds to vest all at once:

Graduated Vesting

Years of Service	Non-Forfeitable Percentage
2	20%
3	40%
4	60%
5	80%
6	100%

Cliff Vesting

Less than 3 years of service - 0% Vested
At least 3 years of service - 100% Vested

Investment Vehicles

Employers who sponsor 401K plans inevitably offer a family of investment funds that can be selected to place both employee and employer deferrals into. These funds are usually administered by a third party investment company that specializes in professional investment services. This can be both a strength and a weakness to 401K plans, since employees are often tied to the exclusive funds that are being offered. Additionally, some companies can legally dictate what funds their matching contributions be invested in while others will offer the employee freedom to choose. Most company benefits managers take periodic steps to monitor the performance and competitiveness of the funds being offered. This is part of their fiduciary duty under the law, ensuring that they are doing everything possible to offer the best retirement plan possible to their employees. Some companies will make matching contributions or profit sharing contributions in company stock valued equally to the required amounts based on current market. This is sometimes done to further incent employees under the theory that good employee performance will enhance stock values and thus benefit retirement plan performance.

All of the provisions outlined above illustrate the many reasons that 401K plans have become the standard retirement vehicle in American business. They are rapidly replacing the old Defined Benefit Pension plans as the standard retirement offering for most employers. 401K plans are a powerful tool to incent and enhance whatever retirement strategies you might develop over your working career. If you have access to a 401K plan it only makes sense that you take full advantage of what the plan might offer from the day you become eligible. To not utilize the strengths such a plan can offer is essentially leaving money on the table, money that could be there for you later in life when you need and want it most.

Roth 401K

Like the Traditional IRA and Roth IRA, the Roth 401K plan allows participating individuals to defer additional monies in addition to pre-tax traditional 401K contributions. Many employers offer a Roth 401K in conjunction with a traditional 401K plan. These plans have to be set up and administered separately. This plan would allow you to defer money in post-tax dollars to the Roth 401K plan over and above and exclusive of any contributions to a traditional 401K. The income you would elect to defer into a Roth 401K plan is not tax deductible. In other words you will still be liable to pay taxes on the income you put into the Roth 401K plan in the year you earned it. However, the investment increase to your account would accrue tax free. When you take a distribution from the plan upon reaching retirement age, there would be no tax liability on that income, since the plan was funded with monies that have already been taxed. The advantage is that all of your investment returns over the years in this plan accrue basically tax free. Another advantage of Roth 401K plans is that they allow considerably larger amounts of your pay to be deferred. The combination of traditional and Roth contributions for a year, including what you defer and what your employer may place in a plan on your behalf, cannot exceed the allowed Section 415 Contribution limits. Rather than the $17,500 limitation of the traditional 401K, these limits were set at $50,000 in 2012. Again, this is a powerful tool, especially as you increase in success and earnings throughout your career.

Employers are allowed to match contributions to Roth 401K plans if they so choose. However, employer contributions are not allowed to accrue tax free and must be placed in a traditional 401K. These funds would be taxed as regular income at the then current tax rate once they are distributed upon retirement.

Section 457 Plans

A section 457 Plan is very similar to a 401K plan, but it is sponsored by city, county, state or federal employers and certain tax-exempt organizations under Section 501(c) of the tax code. Such tax-exempt organizations are most often charitable organizations that are not in business to make a profit, but do have specific operations and career employees. For all intents and purposes, a 457 Plan will look, feel and act the same way as a 401K plan from the perspective of the participants. There are a few differences of note, one of the most prominent being the elimination of an early withdrawal penalty (currently set statutorily at 10% over and above regular income tax rates)if you were to cash out 457 savings before the age of 59½. Also, entities that are eligible to sponsor section 457 plans may also have 401K plans and employees can defer monies into both of them to the maximum allowable under each. Offset rules would not apply between the two plans.

Like a 401K plan, a 457 Plan will undoubtedly be professionally administered with specific investment options and established employer participation. Eligibility requirements are the same as well as the tax consequences of deferrals in reducing your income and reducing your tax liability for monies deferred into the plan. Also, as of 2010, Section 457 Plans also have Roth provisions that allow you to put post tax dollars into an employer sponsored plan. There are a few other technical differences depending on whether the entity sponsoring the plan is governmental or non-governmental, but for the most part these plans are an equally adept method to pay yourself first.

Section 403(b) Plans

A Section 403(b) plan, also called a Tax Sheltered Annuity is a type of savings plan similar to both the 401K and 457 Plan. These plans are available to certain employees of 501(c) 3 organizations (usually recognized as charitable, not-for-profit organizations), certain types of government employees, public school employees and certain classifications of Ministers. These plans allow for the same type of pre-tax contributions to the plan and may include additional matching, discretionary or mandatory contributions from the employer sponsoring the plan. These plans also allow for Roth after tax contributions when specified. One of the main differences between a 403(b) plan and a 401K is that upon retirement, income distribution from the 403(b) must be received in the form of an annuity contract, custodial contract invested in mutual funds or a retirement income account for certain Ministers. These plans also are not subject to certain discrimination tests that other plans must meet. For the most part, these plans still act like a 401K from the participant's point of view and are an equally powerful way to pay yourself first.

Simplified Employee Pension Plan (SEP)

If you are a self-employed business owner, either as a sole proprietorship, partnership, Limited Liability Company or other entity and do not have access to any of the other employer sponsored plans listed above, this might be the vehicle for you. A Simplified Employee Pension Plan, also known as a SEP-IRA, allows you to sponsor your own plan and defer up to 25% of your earnings up to $51,000 per year (2013 limits). This plan can be used for just you as a single employee, or for a small business you have founded that could literally employ hundreds. However, if you are self-employed and have not structured your business in a manner that allows you to be an employee of the business, there are other deduction limits that translate to roughly 20% of the gross income that you must pay yourself out of the business.

Either way, the deferral limits under this plan are many times higher than the standard traditional or Roth IRAs.

Unlike a 401K, the SEP plan only allows for discretionary contributions that are deferred into the plan from business income as a profit-sharing alternative. Voluntary employee deferrals are not allowed. This plan does require identical deferrals for all employees. The plan must designate contributions be made equally for every employee based on a specific formula outlined in the plan. Employer contributions are not mandatory and may be made when and if you decide as a business owner to defer profits into the SEP versus taking them as ordinary income. The only provision is that everyone must receive a similar benefit based on the plan's formula. If you decide to pay yourself 10% of your income in a SEP contribution, everyone else working for you and drawing income from your business must also receive 10% of their wages in plan contributions. There is no discrimination testing for SEP, and administration of the plan is correspondingly simple. The equal benefit rule is the main principle that must be complied with.

Like 401K plans, the SEP can be set up with one or more investment vehicles to invest deferred funds into. This can be through a local bank savings account, a mutual fund company or through a self-directed IRA administrator. As the plan sponsor, you can choose as many investment alternatives as you wish. Also, unlike 401K plans, SEP contributions do not reduce the contribution amounts you can make to traditional or Roth IRAs in addition to the SEP plan. The SEP is an easy and powerful way the self-employed or small business owner can pay themselves first.

The Savings Incentive Match Plan for Employees Individual retirement Account (SIMPLE IRA)

The SIMPLE plan is a relatively newcomer to the retirement plan universe, becoming available in 2005. This plan is geared for smaller employers with up to 100 employees. It has reduced options as to employer matching and contributions to the plan. The SIMPLE plan allows you to contribute up to $12,000 per year of your earnings into the plan ($14,500 if you are over 50). Under SIMPLE plan rules the employer may opt for a dollar for dollar match up to 3% of participating employee's salaries. The employer may also opt not to match employee contributions, but make an annual contribution to the plan of 2% of all employees' wages, whether they opt to participate in the plan or not. While the 3% cap on matches limits the incentives you might have to contribute to a SIMPLE plan, the plan does have the added advantage of immediate 100% vesting for all contributions, employer and employee. As with any employer sponsored plan, this vehicle offers an immediate return on investment through the employer matching funds, thus magnifying any savings you might make into the plan.

Defined Benefit Pension Plans

While some employers and many unions still contribute to pension plans, these plans are slowly disappearing from the retirement planning landscape and being replaced with employee funded vehicles such as 401K plans. A pension plan is a plan that rewards you as an employee or union member for years of service. All monies used to fund a pension plan come from the employer, not out of the employee's pocket. If you qualify for a defined benefit pension plan, you would receive a monthly payment upon retirement based on the calculations outlined in the plan. The monthly benefit is usually calculated based on years of service, final average salary or both. While a pension plan does not technically fall under the principle of paying yourself first, it is important to weigh the benefits you might obtain from such a plan as part of your income replacement once you stop working. Pension plan benefits generally will not come close to equaling final working wages. Pension benefits usually only account for a fraction of the income you would be earning immediately prior to retirement. For example, in 2012 the average pension for all retired New York State employees averaged $31,563 per year, or slightly less than 50% of their average final pay. Obviously, planning and saving with other vehicles outlined above would be necessary to bring income to a level more comfortable to the sustained lifestyle you are accustomed to prior to retirement.

Social Security Benefits

If you look at it from one perspective, Social Security is the government's way of forcing you to pay yourself first. Unlike a 401K plan where the monies deferred are saved directly into an account in your name, social security deducts an amount from your paycheck, currently 7.65% from you with a matching amount from your employer, and pays them into a general fund that theoretically covers all working Americans. The benefit you derive upon retirement is based on a complicated formula, but in no case can it exceed the 2013 maximum of $2,533 per month.

Social Security is a controversial political subject. Actuarial calculations suggest that the monies needed to fund social security are dwindling and that the entire system could be insolvent in the foreseeable future. Changing demographics are resulting in fewer and fewer working people paying into a system that is stressed with a large number of baby boomers retiring. While social security is a benefit that should be considered in an overall plan to pay yourself first, the track record of administration suggests a future benefit may not be a given unless there is serious political and financial change made. In the end, you are still the one responsible to pay yourself first. You cannot ultimately count on the social security system to take that responsibility for you.

Traditional Savings Plans

There is nothing old-fashioned or out of style with a traditional savings plan. Traditional savings are those monies set aside out of a regular after-tax wage that are not earmarked for paying bills or discretionary spending. They can be in the form of traditional bank or credit union savings accounts, investment service money market, bond accounts, stock accounts or any other form you might choose to designate. Personal savings are the epitome of discipline in paying yourself first. The one great disadvantage of these funds is that they are funded with post-tax dollars and all investment income is also taxable year to year. However, unlike tax-deferred savings vehicles, these funds are readily and easily accessible, always straining discipline and providing temptation to spend on either necessities or pleasures. Personal savings should be a goal of every wage earner in order to provide a financial cushion for unforeseen financial events.

An unfortunate dynamic of modern life is the seeming inevitability of unforeseen financial emergencies. It seems that no matter how hard we plan or save, something seems to arise that requires a portion of whatever cash reserves we might possess. The temptation is to more readily prioritize the unforeseen event over the necessity to maintain a healthy savings balance. Using tax-deferred vehicles such as an IRA or 401K adds an effective layer of plan administration that acts as a sort of checks and balances. They are harder to access and come with penalties if distributed before retirement age, therefore providing more incentive to remain in savings and grow with time.

Both traditional savings and tax-deferred vehicles are highly recommended if you can fit them into a monthly budget. You will never look at your personal finances and think "I have saved too much money. I should have spent more." The opposite situation is all too easy and too frequent, where you run out of money before you run out of month. Plan on savings wherever and whenever you are able.

All of the vehicles listed above are available to you. There are few reasons other than personal preference not to employ one or more of these vehicles in order to secure your financial future. You can do it and you must do it in order to sustain your lifestyle beyond your working years. In the upcoming six rules you will come to more clearly understand the why and how of paying yourself first. You will begin to get a clear picture of the fact that you are indeed the master of your own future financial destiny.

Rule 2 – Starting Earlier is More Effective than Starting Later

It only makes sense that the longer you have to invest and the more years you defer monies into a retirement savings account, the more you will end up with when the day to cash your retirement in finally arrives. There are many reasons for this and the main justifications for an early start are outlined in this chapter. The unfortunate reality is that the time of life when retirement savings should most be considered is the time of life few actually think about it. The attractions and opportunities of moving from youth into young adulthood generally do not revolve around concepts of retirement planning. However, that is precisely the time when you can get a jumpstart on a bright future after your working career concludes.

You Can Begin as Early as Age Twenty One to Use Tax-deferred Vehicles

I f most financial experts were asked the question "at what age should someone begin their retirement savings" the answer would universally be "as soon as possible". Most deferred savings vehicles become available to anyone who is eligible to participate by the age of twenty one. At that age, most of us are trying to get out of our parent's home and get serious about college, working on a trade, or working our way along on the bottom rung of a career ladder. The great shame of our educational system as it relates to the realities of our financial culture in America is that at age twenty one we should be made acutely aware of the power of financial planning and the effect time has upon our future. Generally speaking, this is not happening. Almost everyone who plans a thirty or forty year working career should plan on starting retirement savings no later than age twenty five. This is, unfortunately, a time in life where retirement is barely in the consciousness of a young individual departing on a new and exciting career; feeling they have their whole lives and the whole world ahead of them.

We are moving into an age when each of us will have to be more diligent and more personally responsible for our financial future. Time is a powerful asset in the planning and building of wealth. If you truly understand how time can be on your side in building wealth, you will want to get started immediately if you have not already. Time is significant because asset growth and investment return over time greatly magnifies the amounts you set aside in a plan for retirement. Interest and investment return continue to grow over time and the longer the window of time you have, the more opportunity your money has to grow.

Time is also important because it allows the opportunity for the recovery of the inevitable losses that can occur due to economic and market fluctuations. Anyone who has investments in equities can attest to the roller coaster ride the stock market has taken between 2007 and 2012. It is estimated that between 2008 and 2011 over 40% of the net worth of all Americans evaporated in market losses. It takes time and patience to recover from such losses. If a person were retiring in 2014 and saw such losses in their retirement savings, it would be a devastating blow. There is little time to recover from such losses before assets need to be available to replace income during retirement. However, if a person were planning to retire in 2025 such losses, while certainly aggravating and unpleasant, would be less of a cause for concern knowing that a significant time period for recovery and further investment increase was ahead. The length of investment time windows will have a direct effect on retirement planning.

The Later You Start, the More You Must Pay Yourself

It helps to keep the power of time in perspective. Time may seem to be endless when we are young. The future seems to stretch out endlessly before us. But time moves quickly. The years pass in an unexpected hurry. While it may not seem to be a priority to start saving at the very beginning of your wage earning years, each year you delay has a direct effect on the amount of wealth you amass later on in life.

Each year you delay your retirement savings is a year at the end of your working career that you do not have to earn a return on what is hopefully a significant balance. In other words, each year you delay now robs you of a year to build a return on investment later. Stop and think about this for a moment. If you do not start saving $5,000 per year now, it may not seem like much. But forty years from now, that $5,000 could be worth $50,000 and earning a 10% annual return in an investment. So the $5,000 you did not save this year would robe you of $5,000 in investment return towards the end of your working career. Such is the cost of neglecting time.

Further compounding the problem is the fact that if you do not get a fairly early start on savings, you will have to make up for all of the interest and investment returns you might have acquired over the years from new money you earn later in your working career. If you only begin amassing significant contributions beginning in your forties or fifties, you must essentially make maximum annual contributions to have any hope of accumulating significant assets to replace your income upon retirement. You also run the risk of having to lengthen your working years to allow for additional time to earn and save towards the day of retirement.

Such a strategy is not without significant roadblocks to achieving an adequate retirement account. The years of the forties and fifties can be fraught with major expenses. If you are married with children, education expenses are often significant. If you are an empty nester the requirements for adequate savings might impact lifestyle choices such as trips and vacations. Insurance, housing expenses, vehicle purchases and other related capital expenditures tend to increase later in our working years, not decrease. The earlier you begin to save, the more room you may have to breather later on in the last third of your working years if you do not have to increase your contributions substantially to catch up to an established savings goal.

Compound Growth Equals Financial Power; the Advantage of Interest and Time

One of the primary assumptions you must make to get a full perspective of the power of time is that you will experience investment growth in your savings. In other words, the money you save will grow for you through investment returns over time. With the financial crises that have beset many of the developed nations around the globe in the last few years, the assumptions you make may need to be adjusted to reflect financial realities. But you still need to assume that your money will grow and work for you. The more time you have to let that money grow, the more you will have when the day comes to start utilizing it for your retirement. One of the primary benefits of tax-deferred vehicles is that your investment earnings continue to grow unimpeded by taxation.

A simple formula to determine how quickly your money may grow over time is called the rule of 72. This simple formula states that if you take your expected investment return and divide it into the number 72, the product of this formula will tell you how many years until your money doubles. For example, if you assume an annual rate of return of 5% on your retirement savings you can divide 5 into 72 and come up with 14.4. This means your money would double roughly every 14 ½ years. If you assumed an 8% annualized return, 72/8 equals 9 years before your money doubles. Now imagine saving $5,000 into a retirement account at age 25. If you assume a lifelong average of 8% return on your savings, that $5,000 will have doubled to $10,000 by age 34. By age 43 it has doubled again to $20,000. By age 52 it has doubled yet again to $40,000. By age 61 it has increased to $80,000. If you did not start taking a distribution until age 70, the original $5,000 savings has become $160,000 without contributing another dime on your part. That is the simple power of time when looking at potential return on your investments.

Two Case Examples of an Early and Late Saver

Because your money grows at compounded rates, which means that as investment returns grow and remain in your savings account they make more money on the returns already realized, time lost in the early years of your working career means that you have one less year for larger accumulations to work for you at the end of your career. The earlier you begin, the more time is spent growing interest and investment returns within your savings account.

Let us examine an interesting and not atypical scenario. We have two employees of a major corporation, Mr. Alpha and Ms. Beta. At the beginning of our scenario they are both out of college, are the same age at 25 years old, and work in identical positions with identical pay and benefits. Their company has a 401K plan and Mr. Alpha and Ms. Beta have been working for a year and are now eligible to contribute a portion of their earnings to the plan. Mr. Alpha is young, single and enjoys time out with his friends after work and on the weekends. Retirement planning is not the foremost concern in his mind. He spends what he earns with little left over at the end of the month. Ms. Beta has recently been married and hopes to start a family in a few years. She enjoys her career, but her husband is also bright and well educated with a law degree and, having recently been recruited by a large firm, has potentially an even more lucrative future.

Ms. Beta wisely starts deferring $5,000 per year of her salary immediately upon her eligibility in the plan at age 25. The company has a match and contributes an additional $2,500 on Ms. Beta's behalf for a total of $7,500 per year. Ten years later at age 35, Ms. Beta leaves employment to begin her family and does not return to the company. Her total contributions to the plan are $7,500 per year for seven years for a total of $75,000 while working at the company. We will assume that Ms. Beta leaves her money in the company plan to grow and earn investment income until she reaches age 65.

Mr. Alpha, over this same time period, spends his entire income until he finally decides he is going to start using the company plan and defers the same $5,000 beginning at age 35. The company matches his contributions also and he receives $7,500 per year into his account. Mr. Alpha makes the same $5,000 contribution every year for the next 30 years until he retires at the age of 65. The total amount deferred into his account between Mr. Alpha's pay and the company match total $225,000 over that 30 year period.

Assuming a 7% annualized return on each of their accounts, who has more money in their account at age 65? The answer might surprise you as the chart below illustrates:

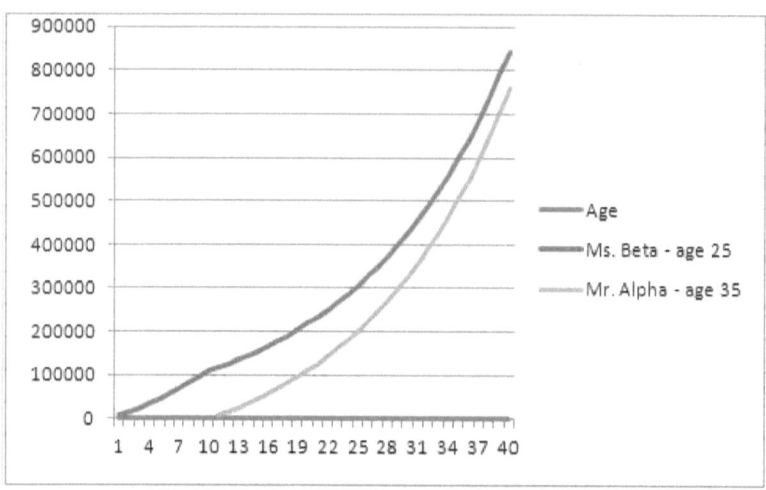

Again, the power of investment earnings over time makes the difference, With Ms. Beta edging out Mr. Alpha even though her out of pocket contributions were a third of Mr. Alpha's over her working career. Assuming that their contribution levels remain at a steady $5,000 per year plus company match, Ms. Beta's balance at age 65 is $844,024 while Mr. Alpha's account is only $758,048. That is a difference of over $80,000 lost to the ravages of time. The performance of the money in the balance of Ms. Beta's account in the ten years prior to her retirement age of 65 makes up for time she did not contribute after age 35.

The next example involves the simple illustration of a personal IRA and the potential risks of procrastination. Let's examine the case of the Omega twins. The Omega twins were born on the same day went to the same high school and college and went into business together for themselves after graduation. We will call them Charlie Omega and Dan Omega (C. and D. Omega). As entrepreneurs with visions of fabulous business and financial success in the future, the Omega twins decide the only planning they need to do for retirement is to open an IRA. C. Omega decides on his 25th birthday to open his personal IRA and begins to deposit $2,000 per year to his traditional IRA account until age 65. D. Omega waits until his 32nd birthday to open his account, and begins at that time to contribute an equal $2,000 per year until age 65. Because of their business skills developed over the years, the Omega twins invest some of their IRA funds in traditional publicly traded stocks and bonds, but put some of their savings into self-directed ventures such as land development and commercial real estate. They end up averaging a 10% per year return over the life of their savings, outpacing the average for publicly traded investments.

The performance of their individual IRAs are illustrated in the chart below.

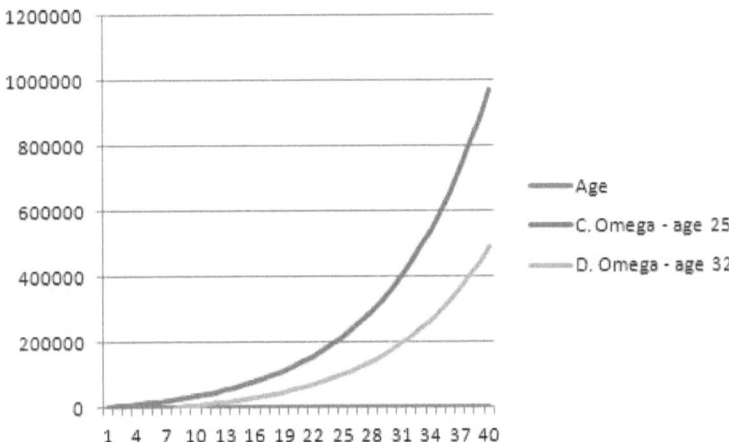

As you can see in the graph above, with the accentuation of solid investment returns, C. Omega's balance at age 65 is nearly double that of D. Omega's. C. Omega will have twice the amount of money upon retirement to enjoy his golden years for simply starting seven years earlier. C. Omega's balance has grown to a healthy $973,703. And this from a minimal $2,000 per year investment. The time frame of forty years and the investment returns realized have yielded C. Omega the greater benefits of time. D. Omega's balance limbs to $488,953. The difference of investment returns over the seven years preceding retirement has robbed D. Omega of the financial benefits realized by his twin brother.

These examples provide clear illustrations of reasoning in dollars and sense. Starting earlier is always a wiser approach and principle than delaying and starting your retirement savings later. No matter what vehicle you choose to plan and fund your retirement, begin as soon as you are able and you will reap the benefits down the road when the appropriate time comes.

Rule 3 – Always Have a Plan

Our lives, at least our financial lives, need to contain a series of identifiable strategies and plans if we are ever to be successful in any specific endeavor. Never has that principle been truer than in planning for retirement. The average working career spans decades and marches relentlessly through a multitude of life phases. Youth and young adulthood melt away quickly into the crowded years of middle age. Responsibilities come and go, but usually become more numbered and more demanding as skills increase over time. Middle age is a time in life where earning potential may be maximized, but the seeming passing of years only seems to arrive ever more rapidly. The retirement years come more quickly than we could ever imagine when we are young and envision an endless parade of unlimited youth, energy and opportunity. In the midst of the marching boot steps of time, it is critical to stop, plan, execute your plan, re-evaluate after a time and plan and execute some more. Time is a fickle mistress in so many of life pursuits, but when anticipated and planned for, time can also become a powerful ally in the strategies of retirement planning.

A Plan Establishes Goals and Direction

One simple fact defines your success in planning for what may be the best years of your life. If you do not formulate a specific plan, you have nothing and are going nowhere. Retirement planning necessitates planning and action. Planning and action suggest that you need to have specific goals and direction. As mentioned earlier, the entire point of retirement planning is to create a goal or series of goals. The main goal should be a specific amount of asset accumulation that will replace your working income once you decide to retire. Call this your specific "magic number" needed to sustain a desired lifestyle once the paychecks cease.

The idea of goals and direction contained in any plan for retirement should contain the how, where what and why of planning that apply to you. Whatever plan you make and however you rethink that plan throughout your working career, the how, what and why of your plan must always have three dynamics in play.

First, the plan has to make sense. The goals need to be realistic and attainable based on the financial realities of your earning power. If your entire household income is $50,000 per year, it is probably not realistic to think you can maximize a 401K contribution of over $17,000 per year. Conversely, if you only put $1,000 away per year for twenty years, you should not expect a very large nest egg come retirement. Further, there will be a number of assumptions you will have to make at many points in time while you are striving to faithfully execute a sound plan. All financial planning involves certain assumptions such as projected rates of return, financial priorities, market conditions and so forth. Many of these critical assumptions will be discussed in later rules, but for now understand that you will have to operate under certain assumptions throughout the planning process. Financial markets are never certain and proper assumptions help to counter the fears and knee-jerk reactions that sometimes occur when markets become volatile. If your plan makes sense, you are much more likely to execute that plan successfully.

Second, your plan must be consistent in terms of goals and execution. If you make a plan, you essentially need to stick with it until such time as reasonable forces of market, employment parameters or time demand that you rethink your strategies. Consistency in outlining a savings and investment strategy and sticking with that strategy are the cornerstones of successful planning. Any strategy or set of assumptions you work under should have that final magic number in mind. You have to pay attention to your plan and touch base with your goals and your plan performance over time. You need to be a willing, consistent and active participant in any plan you undertake.

The third dynamic is fluidity and flexibility in your plan. There is a very distinct tension in being consistent in your planning and making adjustments when necessary. In an age of ever increasing information, change is not only constant it can be much more rapid than in years past. Being able to adjust on the fly when financial conditions warrant is critical in managing your plan successfully. But adjustments should always be made carefully and with proper motive and information while always keeping the final goal and number in mind.

Listed below are the considerations you should establish for the how, what and why of your own personal plan. While every individual will have their own unique circumstances, the issues and question listed below are universal conditions you should include in any plan strategy and execution.

The How of Your Plan

The how of your retirement plan should be focused on how much of your income you plan to use to fund your retirement. Your primary consideration is involved in calculating how much money can be set aside without seriously infringing on your current lifestyle needs. Any employer matches, investment decisions, self-directed initiatives or other strategies you may utilize to fund one or more savings vehicles should be clearly defined. Can you live on an income net of any retirement savings deferrals? Have you figured a lifestyle that will keep your savings at arm's length where it will be able to grow over the entire course of your career without being needed prior to retirement? Again, you need to ultimately establish a magic number that you feel will be able to replace your working income once retired and work the yearly deferral figures accordingly.

The What of Your Plan

You should be able to identify at least one or more specific savings vehicles, either pre-tax or post-tax, to fund your retirement savings. Do you have an employer sponsored 401K, 403b or 457 plan available? Does the employer offer a match? Are you taking full advantage of any monies offered to you through employment opportunities? Can you also use a Roth IRA in conjunction with the plan? Perhaps you have private investments outside of your retirement plan such as savings bonds or income properties that you are relying on. The vehicle or mix of vehicles you chose must be consistent with the assumptions and magic number that you have in mind.

The Why of Your Plan

Remember that the whole idea to establishing and executing a plan for your retirement is to pay yourself first! You need to set monies aside to provide for a time in your life when a paycheck and long work week are no longer possible or desirable. You have to take that responsibility. The why is also to reach for that magic number, a number that reflects an asset accumulation that will realistically allow you to enjoy a specific lifestyle once you are retired. You should always ask "why not take advantage" of every nuance the current tax code allows you to defer monies towards retirement. We have an entire financial industry built around these rules. Why not utilize them to their fullest extent? You should become familiar with and determine to use every possible strategy that your budget supports and the law allows.

Envision Your Retirement Lifestyle and Replacement Income

The whole point of a lifetime of financial planning and discipline is to achieve a goal of financial independence at the end of the road. The idea of financial independence is not a fixed concept. It is as varied as the imagination and dreams of the individual defining it. What does financial independence mean to you? Does it mean being free of debt? Does it mean having enough money to buy a sports car, a boat, to travel, to purchase a second home in a warmer climate? What are the visions you have of yourself, your associations, your surroundings and your activities and adventures once the demands of an everyday career are over? Can you translate that vision into today's dollar values that will be needed to fund that vision down the road? What sort of assumptions will you make about your future? Will it be a time of perfect health? Will there be unforeseen expenses associated with children or grandchildren? Are there hobbies you anticipate taking up that you have not had the time or money for during your career?

A sound plan involves going over the necessities and the luxuries you anticipate as a reality at some point in the future. The next step is to approximate a dollar value for every possible area and nuance of your vision. Finally, what sort of savings and deferrals will it take to get there? How much will you have to take out of your own pocket and how many years will you have to let your savings and investments grow? Is it a safe enough amount? Is your time horizon long enough? If you can dream the dreams, chances are you can formulate a plan that will eventually bring those dreams within reach. Again, it takes discipline and a sound knowledge of the concepts and principles associated with successful planning.

Finding Your Magic Number

The end goal of any retirement plan is to identify what your "magic number" is for retirement and formulate a way for you to reach that number through planning and investment. Your own personal magic number is the value you feel you need to have available upon retirement to enjoy a specific lifestyle. While it is not the scope of this book to create exact formulae for that number it is important to identify the basic framework needed to consider what that number might be and what basic factors need to be considered.. Professional assistance in finding your magic number is highly recommended. There are numerous assumptions that you must make and revisit over the course of a career. Many of the risk assumptions, which will be more thoroughly outlined in Rule 5, need to be regularly revisited and adjusted as market and economic realities require. There are numerous personal preferences that have a likelihood of changing also as you grow, mature and acquire a more seasoned perspective on what necessities and luxuries are important to you.

Nevertheless, there are a few fundamental considerations you need to make when trying to arrive at a rough estimate of what your magic number might be. The simplest calculations center on the age you want to retire and the amount you want available each year to spend. You need to calculate whether or not you can live on the interest, dividends or other investment returns produced by your savings or whether you will need to erode the principal over time. Other calculations are not so easy nor are they necessarily accurately predictable. You should consider your expected life span in years and subtract your expected final age from your retirement age to determine the number of actual years you will need income. Other assumptions such as inflationary costs, discretionary spending needs and set-aside funds for unexpected expenses (such as natural disasters, unforeseen medical problems or family issues)are much more difficult to predict. Identifying what these costs will be is as much guesswork as it is professional prediction. However, trained professionals will be able to show you a number of models that you might utilize to arrive at a number that is comfortable based on your overall expectations and assumptions.

A simple formula for your magic number might look something like this:

Magic Number = Annual Income Needs x No. of Years Expected x Assumptive Risk Factor

Your magic number should be the result of your desired annual income. Calculated in today's dollars, times the number of years you expect to live beyond retirement. This number should be increased by a risk factor that you determine is adequate to cover inflation, unexpected life changes, unforeseen expenses, etc. It would not be unusual to see a factor of ten percent or greater, even to over eighty to one hundred and twenty percent depending on how your expectations of future realities are computed. However you factor in risk and life expectancy, try to define a number that you can be comfortable with. Since no one can entirely and accurately predict the future, finding assumptions that you are comfortable with and will allow you a sense of security is most important.

Use Any and All Available Professional Resources

The retirement planning and investment industries are multi-trillion dollar industries with a veritable smorgasbord of well educated and well trained professionals that can offer almost unlimited resources to assist you in creating and executing a successful retirement plan. Almost every institution that deals in finances, whether investment companies, brokerages, banks, or credit unions, have a department with trained professionals that focus their time and careers on assisting with successful retirement plans. If you work for a company that sponsors a retirement plan such as a 410K, chances are that there is a benefits department or manager that is available full-time as a resource to assist you in taking the greatest advantage of all resources available to you through your employer. The internet is also packed with sites and resources that can provide information and education on almost any issue related to retirement planning. The only thing you need to provide is the motivation to reach out and discover the vast resources available.

There are numerous publications available that can keep you up to date on trends that will affect your money, both form an earnings potential and a savings and investment potential. Publications such as Forbes magazine, the Wall Street Journal, Money and Investing magazine, Consumer Reports, Kiplinger's, Investor's Business Daily and many more are replete with up-to-date information on trends that can have an impact on your savings and investing strategies. Go to your local library and research some of these journals. In combination with internet resources and professional counseling, they form a triumvirate of substantial resources that you may access at almost a moments notice.

One simple word of caution needs to be remembered when counseling with and engaging finance and investment professionals. Most individuals who are highly trained and expert in planning, investing and strategizing for retirement also have something to sell. Whether it is a group of funds being touted as the best vehicle in which to place your hard-earned money, or whether it is a particular expertise that is available on a fee-for-service basis. With the multitude of resources available in the financial universe, with focus and effort you should be able to access professional resources that will educate and enlighten without requiring financial obligation on your part. It is a highly competitive field and your loyalties should be earned, not demanded.

Your Own Research and Education is Critical

Like any other financial concept, the amount of importance you place upon planning for your own retirement will translate into effort in becoming educated on all that you need to know to successfully execute a plan. It is critical that you realize that no one else will do this for you. Despite the wealth and easy availability of resources, you must take the steps necessary to access those resources and learn how to use them profitably. If you are in a career that requires technical expertise to be successful, you will undoubtedly spend the time and effort necessary to remain up-to-date and relevant on those particular skills.

Perhaps it is best to envision your retirement planning as the job inside of your job, the career inside of your career. Although it does not require a tremendous amount of time or effort to plan successfully, it does require some constant time and effort. If you are not developing strategies, creating a plan and monitoring the progress of your plan, you will ultimately not arrive at the magic number you desire. There is no one else with the primary responsibility to make you plan happen. That is part of your personal job description.

It naturally follows that you should avail yourself of educational tools that can help you succeed at your job inside of a job. Investment professionals, professional benefits managers and online resources should be viewed as tools that will help you more efficiently develop and execute your plan. It is up to you to wield these tools in building the best plan to meet your goals and needs.

Periodically Review and Make Adjustments to Your Plan

The only certainty in the world of finance is change. It is also one of the only certainties in your own life over a period spanning a working career. Change is inevitable. Sometimes it can be expected and planned for, but often it involves several unforeseen factors. Your own visions, dreams and tastes will likely evolve over the course of thirty or forty years. Relationships may come or go. Your understanding of the world around you will certainly evolve. What was desirable in your younger years may be irrelevant in your later years. It is probably more the exception versus the rule that a fifty year old maintains precisely the same understanding and expectations of the important touch points of life than they did at age thirty. The magic number for retirement may also change and evolve over time. Risks, economic assumptions, and financial expectations evolve also. A simple example is the performance of domestic stocks in light of the transition to a global economy. Investors must recognize and understand more and varied factors today than they needed to just twenty or thirty years ago. Political philosophies change, conflicts erupt, new global competition emerges, mergers and buyouts occur and companies and concepts that were successful just a short time ago are now obsolete or out of business.

In light of the fast moving environment that is today's world of finance, it is imperative that you touch base periodically with your plan, your goals and your assumptions and consider adjusting your plan based on current circumstances. It is also important to maintain the tension between adjusting your plan periodically and meddling in your plan too frequently. The difference between monitoring your plan too often and just often enough is usually attached to your emotional reaction to market fluctuations. This is a primary reason why a detailed and thoughtful plan, carefully conceived and professionally administered, is necessary to avoid knee jerk reactions to a sudden change in financial markets or investment assumptions. Your goals should reflect a short, medium and long term outcome and it is helpful to monitor each of these time horizons based on your current situation.

With a series of goals attached to your plan, your time horizons will give you perspective that will enable you to weather the short-term setbacks investing sometimes proffers without compromising your long-term outlook. This principle will be examined in detail in Rule 7 as planning and strategy is considered in the light of life phases and time horizons. The principle of periodic plan review is central to your proper management of your plan. It should be undertaken at specific intervals, say every five years for example. Visiting your plan goals and strategies should also be undertaken at times of significant change, such as upon the sale of a business, receiving a windfall or a change in employment. Regular maintenance, usually with professional assistance and guidance, is at the core of prudent planning and management.

Your Strategies Should Reflect Your Plans and Intentions

Your Magic Number is always the goal to keep in mind. The details of your plan in getting to that number should always be reflected in your plan. As your goals change or become modified over the years, so your plan should be adjusted as well. Any assumptions as to longevity, economic risk, investment returns or other factors that you do not necessarily have control of, but must remain aware of, need to be monitored. Your best intentions are to reach your magic number. As that number changes or your pathways and plans to that number need to be revised do not be afraid to act. Also, seek second opinions wherever possible to confirm your intentions and verify that your plan is adequate to meet those financial intentions. The bottom line is this: you plan and your intentions require your care, attention and vigilance. While it is wise to gather expertise around you to assist you in making your plan work for you, the final decision and responsibility ultimately rests with you.

Sample Financial Plan for a Working Professional

Based on our discussion of personal responsibility and executing a sound plan, a simple financial plan for a thirty-five year old working professional is illustrated below. The plan is outlined in levels, with the highest financial priorities in the first levels and each lower level reflecting lower priorities. Your personal financial plan can benefit from prioritizing or "leveling" your regular expenditures. Know where your money is going and what you need it for and want it for. Always keep the top priority to pay yourself first through proper savings vehicles.

Sample Plan for a Working Professional Earning $60,000 per Year

Assumptions:
a) After tax take home pay equals $4,000 per month after taxes and 401K deductions.
b) Mortgage and utilities equal $1,500 per month.
c) Insurance, food, consumer debt, gas and other ancillary expenses equal $1,200 per month.

Level 1 – 6% of gross income into company 401K with a 3% match invested in high growth stocks.
Level 2 – Place $500 per month into liquid savings until a six month savings reserve is accumulated.
Level 3 – Pay mortgage and household expenses. Accelerate mortgage 10% over minimum payment once six month liquid savings is established.
Level 4 – Invest 2% of after tax pay in Roth IRA Mutual Funds using a money market fund.
Level 5 – Invest 3% of after tax pay into college fund invested in Municipal bonds.
Level 6 – Assign $400 per month to discretionary spending/entertainment.
Level 7 – Invest 5% of after tax pay into fast food restaurant partnership.

The above seven level financial plan covers the entire take home pay of $4,000. Yet, it allows you to pay yourself on several levels. It establishes your retirement account first, a liquid savings fund that can act as emergency or "rainy day" funds or part of a major purchase. It also provides discretionary spending, savings for children and high risk investments that may or may not pay off in the future. It also suggests ways to more quickly eliminate consumer debt such as accelerating your mortgage. This is just one of many ways you can establish a plan, diffuse risk in different vehicles and still find time and money to enjoy life along the way. Your plan will be personal to your situation, but whatever your plan might be, in its many iterations over the years, it should have logic, flow, research and reason behind it. And above all, if you truly want to reach your magic number, it must be a plan you are committed to sticking with.

A Few Financial Concepts to Study

Listed below is a table of financial concepts in addition to the plan types listed in Rule 2 that you should research and become familiar with over time. It is not necessary to understand all for these ideas at once, but a gradual self-education as well as professional consultation on any and all of these subjects is advisable if you are to have a solid base of understanding to manage your plan. Each of the subjects below may open doors to additional and deeper concepts associated with the financial world. Remember, your plan is only as solid as your understanding and ability to execute it. These concepts will provide you with a basic foundation of knowledge that will allow you to more effectively and successfully accomplish any plan you might create:

Stocks

Bonds

Money Market Funds

Time Deposits

High Growth Funds

Growth and Income Funds

Balanced Funds

Fixed Income Funds

Partnerships and Limited Liability Companies

Speculative assets (art, jewelry, gold, silver, rare coins, real estate)

Interest Income

Dividend Income

Taxable Investments

Tax Free Investment

Municipal Funds

Cash Equivalents

Fund Administration Fees (load and no-load funds)

Pre-tax dollars

Post-tax dollars

Self-directed Investment Accounts

Fiduciary Duties

Early Withdrawal Penalties

Marginal Tax Rates

Rule 4 – Tax-deferred Investments Always Grow Faster than Similar Taxable Investments

The fact that tax-deferred investments will grow more quickly than investments that must be taxed each year seems fairly obvious. But the real power of tax-deferred savings should be explored and well illustrated to drive home the point that using such tax-deferred growth vehicles is THE most efficient way to pay yourself first and strive to achieve your magic number. Very few people that you know are excited to pay more taxes. Everyone wants to be able to keep and utilize as much of their income as possible. The current tax code in the United States provides well defined avenues for you to do exactly that, keep as much of your income as possible, if you utilize the code properly. The vehicles described in Rule 1 will accomplish tax-deferred growth. It is helpful to see exactly how significant the nature of that growth can be in helping you achieve your goals.

When you are looking down the long road of retirement planning the benefit of not having to tax annual earnings becomes significant. Over the course of a year or two, paying dividend or interest tax will generally not leave a noticeable hole in your savings. But in the course of twenty, thirty or forty years or more, the differences generated by saving that extra portion of your income can be substantial, particularly in the later years of savings when account balances become significant and investment returns are large.

Capital Gains, Dividend, Interest and Ordinary Income Taxes Reduce Your Investment Net Growth

The tax system in the United States is complex to say the least. Careers have been created that focus on creating professional solutions to minimize tax liabilities for their clients as well as assist in accurately reporting and accounting for such tax liabilities. The personal tax preparation industry alone is a multi-billion dollar undertaking. When formulating your personal plan, it is critical to understand the tax implications of certain types of investments and how they impact the actual income you receive on your money. The more you understand the implications of certain types of taxes, the more efficiently you can plan around them as the tax code allows.

Capital gains taxes are the taxes due on the sale of an asset. If you own stock, bonds, mutual funds, real estate or other assets that can be bought and re-sold you will be subject to a capital gains tax on the year in which such assets are sold. The IRS defines a capital gain as:

"Almost everything you own and use for personal or investment purposes is a capital asset. Examples include a home, personal use items like household furnishings, and stocks or bonds held as investments. When a capital asset is sold, the difference between the basis in the asset and the amount it is sold for is a capital gain or a capital loss."

Short term capital gains taxes, defined as those items you have owned less than a year, are treated the same as your regular income tax bracket which is based on your adjusted net earnings. A long term capital gain is defined as an asset you have held for over a year. Long-term gains receive special tax consideration, starting at 0% and increases until it levels out at a 15% level tax rate based on your annual adjusted gross income from all sources. Capital gains tax rates have historically been a highly debated political topic. What you should be aware of is how any gain affects your savings, and how much you stand to gain by harboring any assets that experience a capital gain in a tax deferred or tax free vehicle. Because capital gains are historically lower than regular income brackets, successful investors and planners utilize capital gains liberally in their investment strategies. Stock dividends are treated in much the same way as capital gains, making income on stock investments an attractive source of income for any portfolio. These tax-favored statuses make the buying , holding and selling of stocks, as well as the periodic income from stocks in the form of dividends, attractive investments.

Interest income taxes are the taxes levied on interest income from fixed or variable income savings and cash equivalents. These are normally also taxed at your regular income tax rate. For 2013 the income tax brackets can be as low as 10% or as high as almost 40% depending on your income. A chart of current tax rates is illustrated below:

Rate	Single Filers	Married Joint Filers	Head of Household Filers

10%	$0 to $8,925	$0 to $17,850	$0 to $12,750
15%	$8,925 to $36,250	$17,850 to $72,500	$12,750 to $48,600
25%	$36,250 to $87,850	$72,500 to $146,400	$48,600 to $125,450
28%	$87,850 to $183,250	$146,400 to $223,050	$125,450 to $203,150
33%	$183,250 to $398,350	$223,050 to $398,350	$203,150 to $398,350
35%	$398,350 to $400,000	$398,350 to $450,000	$398,350 to $425,000
39.6%	$400,000 and up	$450,000 and up	$425,000 and up

As you can see, the more income that you make, the more of your investment returns will be paid in taxes each year if you do not shelter them in an appropriate tax-deferred or tax-free savings vehicle. Each dollar you pay each year in taxes on your investment returns could have become several dollars in your retirement savings at the end of your career had they been placed in such a tax-favored vehicle.

Tax-Deferred Vehicles May Include Employer Added Benefits

Of all the benefits that a tax-favored status may provide, employer sponsored plans that provide incentives through matching employee deferrals into the plan provide arguably the best and quickest return on investment. If you work for an employer that contributes $.50 for each dollar you put into the plan you are earning an automatic 50% return on your investment into the plan assuming you become fully vested. Your investment earning power has been increased by that same amount, and a on a tax-favored basis as well. According to the Bureau of Labor Statistics, 61% of all private industry employees have access to some sort of retirement savings plan; include 81% of management and professional position and 41% of service occupations. Public Sector employees have an even higher participation rate.

Among employers who sponsor these plans, matching contributions break down as follows: If your employer matches each dollar you contribute at a rate of $0.50 or less, you are among the majority. Fifty-three percent of employees are in such plans, with many of these offering no matching contribution. Less common are the 9 percent of workers in plans for which the employer contributes $0.51 to $0.99 cents for each dollar the employee contributes, up to a given percent of earnings. The most generous employers match at 100 percent of employee contributions, up to a given percent of earnings. Thirty-six percent of savings and thrift plan participants are in these "Cadillac" plans.

The Tax Game: Assumptions about Present and Future Tax Brackets

One of the main assumptions attached to the benefits of tax deferred savings are the expectations of your tax liabilities, both during the years that you are working and saving and upon retirement. The traditional schools of thought have generally made the assumption that you will almost certainly be in a lower tax bracket upon retirement. Insomuch as distributions of retirement savings are not subject to typical FICA and FUTA payroll tax withholdings like regular earnings during your working years, this is generally true. And most retirement plans do not have an exact dollar for dollar income replacement scenario upon retirement. This is particularly true if the last few years of your career are your highest earning years. Most individual's magic numbers provide a comfortable level of replacement income, but usually not the highest working income realized during peak earning years. However, tax codes change through various political administrations and assumptions that may have held years ago are not necessarily as true today.

For most individuals, your tax rates should be expected to decline during your retirement years. But this assumes a consistent and level tax code between now and the time you retire. Increases in tax rates would obviously require a change in your strategies and thinking. And the fact is that the only consistent assumption you can make is to operate under the present tax system structure. Federal and state tax structures are as much political as they are practical, and no amount of guesswork can accurately predict the future. All that really exists is the tax code as it now stands. And these are the assumptions you can and must most accurately use. If a subsequent Congress makes changes to tax rates, you have to re-evaluate and make any necessary changes to your plan accordingly.

When evaluating the spending power of your magic number, tax assumptions are best calculated at current rates based on your expected annual distribution income. But as each subsequent administration examines the income and spending needs of the country, expect to change your assumptions if and when the tax brackets change. As always, there is plenty of professional help available to aid you in integrating tax assumptions into your overall plan. You simply need to stay on top of the game.

The Simple Power of Pre-tax versus Post Tax Dollars

The bottom line for using tax-deferred savings plans in order to pay yourself first is found in the simple value of pre-tax versus post-tax dollars. Keep in mind that a dollar saved before it is taxed is worth more than a dollar saved after you have paid taxes. It is simple math. Let's assume that you are in a 25% income tax bracket, including federal and state income tax. Under this realistic scenario every dollar that you earn actually has only seventy-five cents worth of purchasing power. If you are establishing post-tax savings, you would actually only have seventy-five percent of every dollar that you earned available to pay bills and to fund a savings account. Simply put, taxes erode your spending power.

Under the same scenario, if you are deferring savings into a tax favored vehicle, such as an IRA or 401K plan, the monies used to fund these savings vehicles are pre-tax dollars. This means that 100% of the monies deferred are put into the savings vehicle before any taxes are removed. The purchasing power of each dollar is worth exactly one dollar. This may be a further benefit via the fact that tax-deferred savings actually lower your gross pay by the amount you put into such vehicles. In some cases, this may actually reduce your earnings to the point it lowers your tax bracket, thereby making each post-tax dollar you receive a bit more valuable. If the tax scenario above were to apply, it would take roughly $1.34 of post-tax earnings to equal the same amount of savings you would realize for each dollar of pre-tax monies you save. Pre-tax dollars greatly extend the savings value, and thus the financial power, of each dollar that you earn. If you are going to experience the greatest benefits from paying yourself first, make sure you pay yourself with the most valuable assets you can, pay yourself with pre-tax dollars.

In addition, if you earn an investment return on your savings, these funds also will be eroded at an amount equal to your tax bracket if they are not earned in a tax-favored vehicle. This decreases the cumulative power of your savings over time, as each dollar paid in taxes, whether it be interest income, dividend income or capital gains, is a dollar not available to earn a return into your account in future years. One of the significant benefits to using tax-favored vehicles is that it allows the earnings on your savings to grow without being taxed each year.

The more you earn on your savings, the more the compounding value of those returns increases over time. This is illustrated in the chart below. This chart shows the value of saving an initial one-time sum of $5,000. Without any other additional contributions on your part, the balances are calculated under the assumptions that you put one sum into a tax-deferred vehicle and the other into a taxable investment. A total of 31% in taxes is assumed in the post-tax example. This example also assumes you earn an 8% annualized return each year.

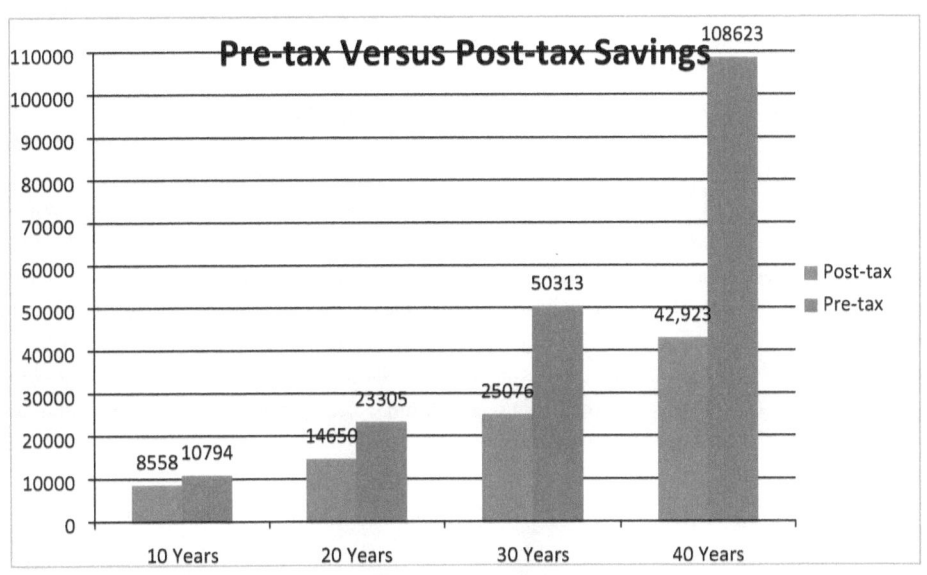

As you can see the value of your savings in pre-tax dollars is $ 23,305 after 20 years, while your post tax savings only has a balance of $14,650 over the same period. At the end of forty years, the pre-tax account has more than double the value of the post-tax account, posting a margin of $108,623 versus $42,923. The difference of $65,700 is the value you received simply by establishing a tax favored account. As you can see, over time the difference is significant. Also keep in mind it would cost you up to $1.34 of earnings value based on your tax bracket to fund the post tax account, which compensates for the fact you will pay taxes on the tax-favored account once you start taking distributions while not being taxed in the future on the post-tax savings. The advantage is still clearly to the tax-favored account. Pre-tax savings dollars simply go further and offer more savings power to you over time. In almost every case it is to your advantage to utilize pre-tax savings vehicles in your overall plan to pay yourself first.

<u>Rule 5 – Risk is Usually Related to Return</u>

Risk is more than just a term everyone who creates a retirement plan must understand on an intellectual basis. Risk is a life philosophy. It is a state of mind that influences every decision we ever make. How you feel about risk and how you tolerate the fluctuations risk can bring will continually shape your life decisions, especially investment behavior. Understanding what risk is and what it implies is the first step in managing the ever present risk in your plan. Living and experiencing risk and taking control of your reactions to risk is a key to executing any plan effectively.

Risk is simply defined as a mathematical probability that any investment you undertake can lose value. The greater the probability that an investment might experience a downturn in value, the greater the associated risk. The traditional mindset has always been that the more risk you take, the more return you should realize for taking that risk. As a general rule, this principle has historically held true. Of course, there are always plenty of exceptions to such rules. In a very real sense, investing is not dissimilar to trying to divine the future. Investments that should be low risk and modest return can sometimes payoff very well. Or at times, supposed low risk investments can offer periods of negative returns or fail completely. Consequently, many high risk investments may return very little or lose value very quickly when a high return might have been expected. For the most part however, investments that have less risk involved generally do not offer the returns higher risk investments may offer. Low risk investments tend to be less volatile and more predictable, but less lucrative. High risk investments tend to be more volatile and have potential for both higher return and higher loss. However, studying different types of risk and being educated about markets and overall business dynamics and principles that might affect your investments is only the beginning. You must also be honest with yourself and how you will react to risk and risk-laden events when they occur.

<u>Identifying and Understanding the Most Common Types of Risk</u>

What you must understand as the individual most responsible for your own plan and your own success is that risk can be learned and understood only to a degree. You can understand the nature and possibilities that risk brings, even if the specific negative events associated with respective types of risk cannot always be foreseen. The more you know about risk, what causes it and how you will react to it, the more successful you will be in incorporating factors of risk into your basic plan. In order to better get a handle on risk, it is helpful to examine some of the major categories of risk. You need to understand the most common categories of risk and think through how such risks might impact your investment choices and overall plan. You must also reflect on how such risks might affect your behavior in managing your plan. As with any technical concept listed in this book, you should broaden your own education on the subject and then confer with experienced professionals that you trust to provide detailed insight into the subject. The types of risk listed below are the most common factors to be aware of and become familiar with.

Systematic, Market or Economic Risk:

This broadest concept of risk refers to a system-wide problem such as a widespread economic downturn, war, political upheaval, shortage of natural resources or commodities, natural disaster or other risk that may affect any and all potential investments within large groups of industries. It is almost impossible to strategize against this type of risk since it affects almost everyone and everything that generates income. For example, the 9/11 bombings of the World trade Center sent powerful ripples through the entire economy of the United States, and inevitably the world, for some time after the event's occurrence. So also did the financial crisis of 2008.

Unsystematic Risk:

This type of risk affects one specified area of the economy or the private sector. It is financial risk based on the changing parameters associated with a certain company or industry. A simple example is the dot com bubble that burst in 2001. Many investments in internet companies took strong hits in value during these periods of downturn. While the entire economy might have sagged bit during this time, there were positive areas that were not directly affected by the risks and downturns this specific industry was confronted with. Another example might be the Gulf of Mexico oil spill. Because of the public perception and costs of cleanup, BP Oil suffered a strong temporary devaluation until that particular crisis had been put behind them. All types of specific risks may fall under the general categories of systematic or unsystematic risk.

Default or Credit Risk:

This risk refers to companies or government entities that may experience a reduction in income to the point that they cannot repay their current obligations. If you are invested in corporate or government bonds or mortgage backed securities that are dependent on reliable payment, any default will obviously impact your return. The financial crisis of 2008 was spurred in large part by widespread credit defaults on certain types of securities.

Inflation Risk:

This is an obvious type of risk associated with the fluctuation in currency values and the buying power of the dollar as tied to inflation. If inflation is higher than your return on a certain investment, the net buying power of that investment is actually losing value, not gaining. An example is the fixed income return offered through certificates of deposit. With interest rates as low as they have been since 2011, certificates of deposit have actually had a negative inflation adjusted return for over two years. In other words, the buying power of a dollar is fading faster than certain fixed income investments can earn in a given year.

Country or Sovereign Risk:

This risk describes the inability of a specific country to be unable to meet its financial obligations. Governments issue debt instruments to pay for their operational functions and rely on future taxation to repay these instruments. If debt levels exceed a government's ability to repay or their tax revenues drop sharply, say from a recession, the very solvency of the nation and all of their debt is threatened. Recent uproars in Greece or Cyprus illustrate the volatility that can occur when governments are threatened with insolvency. Debt issues in European and Asian countries and even the United States make Sovereign risk a real factor to consider when investing.

Currency/Exchange Risk:

Investments in vehicles that include interests in entities outside of the United States, such as an International Equity Fund, must deal with constant fluctuation in the currency exchange rates. Weakened currencies or dramatic shifts in exchange rates between the country in which an investment is place and the U.S. dollar can dilute your rate of return. Consequently, shifts in exchange rates in your favor enhance your return, which is one reason international funds are popular when such circumstances are favorable.

Interest Rate Risk:

This risk applies mainly to bonds and fixed income investments. As interest rates change so do the yields of investments sensitive to those rates. Expected returns can be diluted with an unfavorable change in interest rates that lowers a bond yield or lowers the return of a fixed income vehicle. For example, many fixed income investments are so low due to the extraordinarily low interest rates of the past few years that their yield to inflation is actually negative.

Political Risk:

Political risk involves the effect political decisions might have on certain industries. In most countries, governments have the regulatory power to allow specific industries to thrive or to be limited based upon applicable legislation. If you have investments in industries that are subject to tighter government restrictions or other legislation that may impact the profitability of companies engaged in affected industries, your investments may decline due to mandated changes in their business practices. For example, when legislation addressed perceived weaknesses in Wall Street after the economic crash of 2008, business practices and profits were affected across a broad array of banks and investment companies due to the new regulatory environment.

Liquidity Risk:

Many investments are bought and sold within applicable market timing. The maxim "buy low sell high" applies in any type of investment scenario. When an investment has a limited market or uncertain time frame in which to be sold, this in known as liquidity risk. Real estate is a good example of this type of risk. The time to sell of an investment may not be equal to the time frame of the best opportunity to sell. If there are fewer buyers than sellers of a certain type of investment, you may have to sell it at a discount. Any investment that cannot be bought or sold quickly poses an additional level of risk due to it relative lack of liquidity.

Operational or Business Risk:

If you have invested in the stock of a specific company and that company has poor operational performance, the value of your investment may decline sharply. If companies do not respond to market conditions, competition, personnel issues or plan for the future sufficiently they can experience a variety of operational problems, all of which diminish the company's performance and result in your investment losing value.

Valuation Risk:

A great skill to investing is learning what investments are a good buy with future earnings prospects. You can never be exactly certain how a certain stock, bond, piece of real estate or other investment will actually pan out. You can only do your research and make your best guess. Valuation risk is the risk of buying an investment at a price that may be overstated for what its future value or return might be. The recent public offering with Facebook is a fine example, their stock having lost significant value from its offering price and owners of the stock still hoping to see the value of their investment equal or exceed the initial asking price.

Concentration Risk:

Placing a majority of your investment dollars in one specific company or industry poses serious risk should that one entity experience a downturn. Concentrating on one specific narrow area of investment, even if you may know it well, can pose a risk. Investing in many different areas, known as diversification, can offset the risk of having a portfolio that is too narrowly focused.

Technology Risk:

There is always risk involved when a company you are invested in loses ground based on new technologies that render their core businesses obsolete. Anyone invested in news media companies such as magazines or newspaper publishers has seen the results of this risk over the last decade. Internet technologies and changes in the way we obtain and disseminate information have strongly impacted staple businesses that were industry standards for decades. In most businesses today, new technologies are a moving target. Guess well and you may profit; stay attached to waning technologies and you will certainly lose.

Volatility Risk:

With many investments, especially the world of stocks, values can fluctuate periodically and can experience rapid peaks and valleys at any given type depending upon systematic occurrences. Volatility can be detrimental if you have a short investment window and are expecting to cash out an investment in a period where values are falling rapidly.

Reinvestment Risk:

When certain investments mature, such as bonds or time deposits, there is always the chance that they may not be able to be rolled over into a vehicle that offers similar returns. A lack of available comparable vehicles in which to put your money forcing you to rethink that part of your plan poses a risk.

Mortality Risk:

Some investments come in the form of periodic payouts, such as an annuity. These payments are often calculated based on life expectation. If you were to pass away before the full payout of your investment was realized, this would be known as mortality risk.

Personal or Emotional Risk:

There is always the unknown of your own feelings and expectations. How you perceive certain risks or what your research tells you about a certain investment will undoubtedly influence your behavior. There is always the risk that your feelings or the information you receive will not result in the most effective and logical behaviors. You take a personal risk every time you invest in something. You can never be right every time or wrong every time. Your emotional discipline is always a risk as you attempt to formulate, evaluate and adjust your investment strategies.

Risk and Diversification

There are few investment professionals today who would not tout the virtues of diversification. Diversification is simply defined as spreading your investments, and thus the risks associated with those investments, among many different types of vehicles. Stocks, bonds, fixed income vehicles, real estate, private partnerships and so on all have potential for returns and potential for trouble. Spreading your investment risk across many varied investments helps to ensure that if one part of your portfolio does not perform well, other investments have the opportunity make up for it.

Diversification itself poses some minor risks. The more types of investments you choose, the more you may need to research in broad and diverse financial subjects to feel comfortable and confident. Diversification is a specific discipline for investment professionals and it is always wise to engage professional help when making a higher strategic decision such as how best to diversify your portfolio. There are seemingly unlimited types of investments and funds available and your choices will often be broad and varied.

Mutual Funds are widely used and popular in today's investment world. These funds attempt to create a diverse investment mix revolving around a specific investment philosophy. In other words, mutual funds use experienced fund managers and a core philosophy to choose a mixed variety of individual investments that fit that philosophy. As an investor, you are removed from researching each specific investment in the mix. You only need to study the strategic direction, philosophy and history of the fund. Mutual funds exist in every popular investment niche. You can choose stock funds that are designed for high growth, for growth and income, for high income yields, for specific technologies, for specific industries and so on. You can choose corporate bond funds, municipal bond funds and fixed income funds. These are usually categorized as to risk and return or follow certain industry trends. For example, high yield bond funds for middle sized young companies are popular. They differ from bond funds invested in blue chip companies which differ from bonds issued by municipal entities and so on. There is no lack of ways to diversify your investments. You just need to be proactive, contact an investment professional or your employer specialist, turn on your computer and start looking and learning.

What you need to remember is that, as a general rule, diversity in your investments spreads risk of loss across a wider umbrella of investments. The idea is that if one fails, others may prosper. Diversification is no guarantee of investment success, but it is a sound strategy for limiting your exposure to specific types of risk.

Risk and Investment Time Horizons

Your perspective of risk should be directly influenced by the type of time horizon you are dealing with. The amount of time you have between the present and some future date, at which time you will want to access your savings, is known as your investment window or horizon. Obviously, if you are looking at a longer window of time you have more room to suffer through the ups and downs various investment risks and market cycles will inevitably impose upon your portfolio. If your window of time is short, it is generally wise to start moving money into vehicles with less volatility to preserve the capital you have accumulated. If your time horizon is medium to long, the volatility that riskier investment might bring may not be as concerning since there should be plenty of time to cycle out of a down market and back into growth and profitability. The last decade has exhibited plenty of volatility. Stocks went into a free fall in 2008 and 2009. If you were on a very short time horizon and had a large investment in stocks, you may have lost over half of the value of your portfolio. But since the lows of 2009, the market has more than doubled. Investors with longer horizons would have been restored the majority of losses they experienced and are likely even further ahead today. Who knows where there investment will be in another five to ten years; or twenty years or more.

Volatility and time go hand in hand. If you have invested in a fund that rises 37% in one year, you will be quite pleased at your success. If that same fund dropped 20% the following year you would probably feel some regret over the investment. If, in the following third year, the investment went up another 15% you would look at the medium term performance of the fund as a success, having realized a strong positive return of 26% throughout the three-year period. The longer you extend the window of time, the more you are able to suffer through the up and down cycles that comprise the volatility of any investment.

The general principle is this: the longer your time horizon for investment and growth, as it relates to an end date where you will actually start relying on your savings, the more both your perception and tolerance of risk will be more acceptable. With personal relationships time can be a healer of all wounds. In the investment business, time is almost always on your aside assuming you have plenty of time to play with. At least, historically, this is the way investments markets have always worked. We must assume that trend will continue despite the changing landscapes of national and global economies.

Risk and Historical Performance

This disclaimer is almost universal in any disclosure having to do with investment: "past performance is not a guarantee of future results. " The only thing constant in this world, especially when it comes to investing, is change. The types of risk discussed in this chapter attempt to address various forms of change in operational, political and market conditions that might affect your investment plan and perception of risk. If there is one assumption you must ever be cognizant of it is that risk, both real and perceived, of the continuing performance and prosperity of any investment choice is always in play. In an ever expanding and changing global market place, the ground can shift quickly under any investment if certain risks are encountered. Despite this ever present market reality, there are sets of assumptions you can and must work under to execute any coherent plan.

First, you must assume that past trends of historic activity will tend to be repeated in future investment activities. Stocks have always outperformed bonds and other fixed income investments and so forth. At least if you take broad enough strokes of time into consideration. If you have a long range plan you need to seriously consider how investment returns have fared in the past. There is a high probability that the same correlations will be realized in the future, even if such guarantees are not iron clad.

Second, you must also assume that change is constant. Exactly how, in what areas and in what form that change will come can never be entirely certain. The one certainty is that there will always be change. These broad and specific changes are good enough reasons in themselves to always subject your plan to periodic review and professional counseling. No one is able, whether as a casual investor or an engaged professional, to identify and predict every change that occurs in the marketplace. But careful attention, periodic review and proper professional counseling can mitigate these changes to a significant degree. You must be diligent in both questioning and addressing the risks and assumptions of your plan in light of change that may affect the future performance of that plan.

The chart below show the historical performance of three main investment types over a long-term time period. The chart shows the increase in value of $1.00 over a seventy year period beginning in 1925. What assumptions or conclusions can you take from these charts? Do the relative consistency (or inconsistency depending on your point of view) of the investment mean anything to you based on your own feelings toward investing? What implications would such information hold for you and your feelings toward risk and expectation of return? Might the future look the same? What might cause the future to look different?

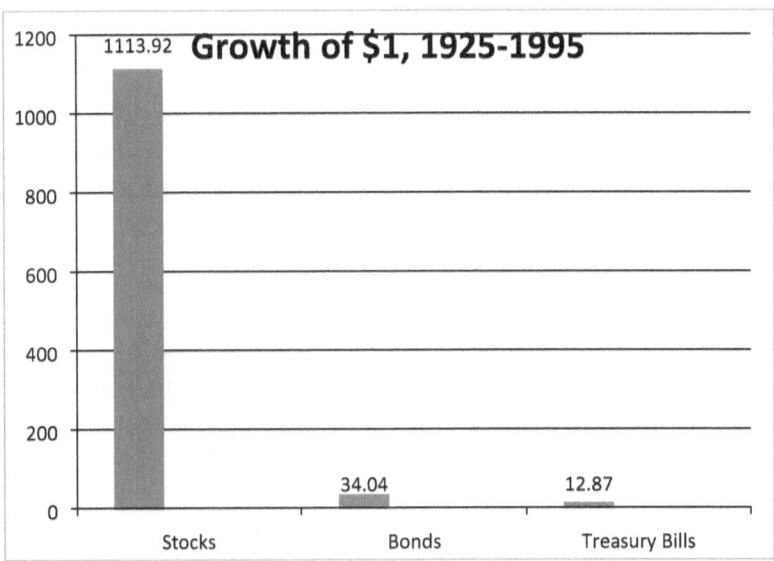

As you have seen in this chapter risk is a broad and very real presence that will have a constant impact upon your retirement plan. While specific types of risk are easily identifiable and are readily able to be addressed, the more unpredictable dynamic is how you will react and behave in the presence of such risks. In the next rule we will look at the necessity of being able to not just identify risk, but live comfortably with the risks you have chosen. History is a relentless instructor on the values of risk and return. But more important than the hard numbers are the subjective feelings you have regarding risk and how you will act to either embrace or avoid the implications risk and volatility bring to investing.

Rule 6 – Determine the Acceptable Level of Risk and Live with the Returns

While the last rule described various types of risk you should become familiar with, this rule focuses more on your feelings and behaviors regarding risk. Taking risks implies a degree of pressure. Pressure to ride out the up and down cycles that many investments will take. Pressure to make decisions based on perceptions of risk, whether real or imaginary, that will directly affect your future plans and outcomes. Pressure to make certain assumptions and live with them. Pressure to try and know as much as you can in advance about the many factors that might affect your investments. All of these pressures can overwhelm an individual investor without proper perspective and discipline.

Your perspective on risk will directly affect your behavior toward risk and the impositions risk will make on your retirement plan. You can count on specific events occurring over and over through the years that will have a negative impact on your investments. Likewise, there will be many events over time that positively affects your investments. Your perspective and personal ability to maintain balance, plan properly and have confidence in your plan and strategies will serve you well in the long run. Whatever attitude you adopt towards the risks that face your investment plan, make sure you are comfortable with the plan and strategies you have made. Remember that investing for retirement is a marathon, not a sprint. Your comfort levels with your decisions will take pressure off of you when markets are not behaving in ways that meet your expectations or positively impact your investments.

Determining Your Personal Investment Philosophy

It is important that you take a good look at yourself from day one of retirement planning and seek to establish your own personal investment philosophy. Your attitude and ability to learn and develop an informed perspective will greatly influence your personal philosophy. You have to ask yourself a series of questions and accumulate enough knowledge and understanding to be able to honestly answer some very personal questions about risk. Can you tolerate risk? Can you adopt a long-term perspective? What are your expectations of investment growth? Are your expectations in line with market realities? Can you foresee how you might react if certain market trends or investment experience do not turn out as you had envisioned? Will you panic? Have you truly studied various investment vehicles and understand how they react to rising and falling markets? Will you react emotionally or seek balanced, alternative and professional perspectives? In other words, you need to be honest with yourself about how such experiences might affect you. If you establish and understand your personal philosophy and tolerance for risk, you are more likely to live within the parameters of a reasonable plan. You are more likely to entertain proper perspective in times of falling market trends. You are less likely to make knee-jerk emotional responses at precisely the wrong time. A clear and strong personal investment philosophy helps you avoid improper emotional behaviors in reaction to changing markets.

Beware of Bad News, Cautious of Good News

Research, education and professional assistance are all recommended as you develop your own personal investment philosophy. One legitimate reason to become as informed as possible is to be able to sift through the volume and nature of information that is available. We live in an era of media saturation. Television, radio, magazine and newspaper media must compete with seemingly unlimited internet resources for your time, attention and dollars. One traditional trend that media has always utilized to attract your attention is sensationalism. By creating a frenzy or panic over an issue, media attempts to attract your attention and viewership. This applies to the world of finance and investing as much as any industry.

The pipers of bad news are always sounding off. Creating a potential crisis when it comes to markets, investing and finance is a sure way to attract the attention of viewership. A recent Pew Research Center study showed that when it comes to finance and investing stories that involved both good and bad news ranged between 30% and 68% depending on market conditions. Stories that contained mostly bad news ranged between 24% and 80% depending on market conditions. Curiously, stories involving mostly good news ranged only between 1% and 11% of all news stories. The moral of the story…bad news sells. Reaction to bad news, no matter how credible the sources might seem, should be tempered by the stability of a long term view of your plan and your philosophies. Beware the doomsayer, for they are rarely accurate and frequently incorrect. And they always have something to sell, usually seeking to purchase your allegiance to their doom saying.

On the other hand, be cautious the eternal optimist. Many investment professionals have a tendency to paint a rosy picture of their fund's performance and tout the most favorable historical numbers. It is natural to downplay risk when competing for investment dollars, as emphasizing the negative is almost always bad salesmanship. Keep a fair and balanced mindset when developing your own philosophy. Things are probably never as bad as they seem and never as good as they seem. The potential realities that lay somewhere between these two appearances should be the object of your focus, research and philosophy.

Risk Averse and Risk Taking Behavioral Patterns – Ten Types of Investor Styles

Your honest assessment of your behavior as it relates to risk should directly shape your overall investment plan and philosophy. There are many different styles and approaches to investing. Your particular tastes, expectations and tolerance of risk likely fit you into one of many common investor styles base upon your behavioral patterns. Illustrated below are ten types of investor styles that are familiar to most investment professionals. Which type of investor most accurately reflects how you see things? What might the best investment philosophy, whether conservative, moderate or aggressive, based on the type of investor that you identify with? What does your most accurate type say about your tolerance of risk?

The Marionette: This type of investor tends to consider themselves inexpert in anything financial. They tend to defer to any advice from someone they perceive as more informed or more professional. The problem with this type is that they are not clear on how they personally view their portfolio and the risks associated with it. Just like a real string puppet, if the strings of their expectations are cut by investment decisions determined by others, they may not know how to move or act otherwise. Fear of learning or fear of failure may provide negative motivation for this investor type.

The Gambler: The gambler likes to play the odds and hit the long shot. Gamblers actually enjoy trying to pick a big winner out of a field of also-rans. Gamblers may not blink at one investment losing money if other investments are hitting it big. Gamblers view the whole investment world as a big game. They are determined to buck the odds and beat the house. Gamblers also like to find investments that are out of the ordinary and overlooked by others. Gamblers will spend the time and effort to try and find the next winner to lay odds on.

The Wizard: The Wizard is an investor who considers they have special insight, whether generated by their own research or outside professional advice, into investments that contain some sort of extraordinary and special potential. They attempt to conjure magical results from investments that may or may not have the potential to offer the returns they expect. Unfortunately, if Wizards break their magic wand on the stone of market realities, they can become frustrated and leave the game or allow it to play out by itself.

The Accountant: The Accountant is calculating, deliberate and conservative. They want the numbers to line up neatly in the columns and do not like unexpected surprises. Accountants are as deliberate and analytical as necessary. But they want practical and tangible results regularly. If an investment does not add up, they are likely not interested. Accountants do not like most risk, risk does not add up to positive dividends in their mindset and no accountant likes red ink.

 The Mechanic: the Mechanic prefers a hands-on approach to investing and likes to be involved in every step of the process. If things are not running well they like to tweak, tinker and re-tune their portfolio as often as necessary to keep it running smoothly. Mechanics need to be cautious that too much tinkering might wear out a few pieces or strip the bolts of their investment plans and long-term goals. Mechanics need to remember that when something is running smoothly, further tuning may not help.

The Prima Donna: Prima Donnas enjoy focusing on one particular type of investment or investment approach simply because it is popular or widely touted as the latest and greatest thing. A Prima Donna would enjoy telling friends and colleagues of the unique success of their particular investment fetish. But if their preferred philosophy fails them, they will shrink from the spotlight. Prima Donnas need strings of successful investment hits to keep them interested in performing their next act. Without consistent and positive reviews, they can burn out quickly.

The Scientist: The Scientist is the analytical monster who tends to research, experiment, and re-run the tests on any given investment or philosophy. Scientists tend to be skeptical of any investment that cannot demonstrate tangible results on a consistent basis. Scientists will expect that if an investment has worked well in the past, it should work equally well in the future. Scientists are disappointed and confused if their empirical expectations are not realized. But scientists also tend to find consistent results through their careful research, even if an experiment or two fails to produce.

The Farmer: The Farmer is a conservative soul that likes to plant his investment ideas and see steady, regular growth. He wants his portfolio to sprout and grow tall within the predictability of a pre-determined growing season. The Farmer is averse to any storms or pests that might eat away at his crop, and hopes to harvest every dollar he has invested in the soil of his portfolio. The farmer lives by the predictability of the seasons and prepares well in advance for rain, snow or sunshine in the investment markets.

The Chef: The Chef is a creative but reasonable investor. The Chef takes a number of diverse ingredients and creates a dish that he expects to be pleasing to the palette. If one particular combination of ingredients does not work out the way the Chef wants, he will try a few new twists to the recipe. The Chef welcomes the diversity of ingredients and tastes as part of his professional palate. If the chef experiments long enough, he knows he may end up creating a new culinary masterpiece, even after a few attempts that resulted in mediocrity.

Your particular research, education and feelings will inevitably shape your portfolio. It is best to be realistic with your type, philosophy and tastes, particularly when it comes to behavior surrounding risk. The reality is that most investments have some sort of risk associated with them that will affect the rate of return they are able to provide. Whether that involves a decreased rate of return of a negative rate of return depends on the potential volatility of the investment. Your particular style should recognize the constant presence of risk based on how you will realistically react.

Let's consider the case of Mr. Theta. Mr. Theta is a young professional with a college degree. He has been working at an engineering firm which hired him out of college for five years and participates in their 401K plan. Mr. Theta has never really studied his investment philosophy and simply checked options on investment funds with his benefits department when he initially signed up for the plan. After speaking with a Benefits Manager, he initially places 80% of his portfolio in stock mutual funds of various types with 20% in bonds and fixed income investments. He makes these choices simply by viewing historical returns of each fund on a handout available to all employees. A few years later, during a rather sharp and volatile market downturn, Mr. Theta looks at his quarterly benefits statement and sees that his portfolio value fell 18% over the last quarter due to global financial unrest. The following Monday Mr. Theta visits his benefits department and changes his investment mix to 90% fixed income vehicles. After a year, Mr. Theta sees that his portfolio has increased in value by 2%. Over the same period the stock market has rebounded. Had Mr. Theta left his investment mix alone, his portfolio would have recovered his losses and increased an additional 9%.

Mr. Theta's case illustrates precisely the emotional behavior that can occur without a solid investment philosophy and understanding of your personal type and style. If you do not understand risk and how you personally would feel and react to risk, it is not unusual to take actions that are the opposite of what might be the best course of action during market volatility. Establishing your personal investment philosophy gives you a foundation of calm amidst the storms of everyday investment experience.

Taking a Personal Risk Profile

It might be helpful if you have not established your own personal philosophy to take a brief quiz to gauge how you really feel about risk. Below are twenty-five basic questions. Take a moment and answer them as honestly as possible. It would be helpful to take a pencil and piece of paper and write down each answer in sequence. After answering the questions, refer to the test key to determine in what range your personal feelings and philosophies might fall.

Personal Risk Profile:

Answer True or False to each question below. Keep track of your answers by writing down a T or F for each question. Answer honestly according to your feelings and perceptions right at this moment.

1) I do not worry if there is no insurance or guarantee on my investments.
2) It is better to tolerate a short-term loss of principal if I can realize a higher return in the long run.
3) I have ten years or more to invest before I need to have replacement income for retirement.
4) All types of investment pose some level of risk and I am clear on the basics of what those risks entail.
5) If I know I can get stronger returns, I am willing to put all of my savings at risk for loss of principal.
6) Any investment return below 8% per year is substandard and is unacceptable.
7) I have no control over markets thus I do not ultimately have control over my investment experience.
8) Investments that return less than 5% per year do not hedge inflation and reduce my long-term return.
9) I do not mind if my savings investments are not liquid for long periods of time.
10) I like to see my savings grow quickly and explosively as often as possible; those are real results.
11) Slow, steady and predictable investment returns are simple, unexciting and for the faint of heart.
12) If you know what you are doing, you can consistently beat the market averages in your portfolio.
13) I like to find investment opportunities that others have not thought about.
14) Anyone with a computer and a few financial contacts can figure out how to outpace the market.
15) I never need more than a few months liquid cash in savings to meet my needs; I put money to work.
16) Retirement savings are a long-term proposition with the flexibility to gamble in the short run.
17) Regular markets may not offer the types of returns that self-directed opportunities allow.
18) Limited Partnerships, Commercial Real Estate Development and other creative business endeavors would make an excellent cornerstone of any portfolio with the right time horizons.
19) If you try to time the market with stock purchases and sales, you can realize strong short term gains.
20) An annual return on your portfolio below 12% cannot be considered very aggressive.
21) Fluctuations in national and global economies should be seen as an opportunity, not a risk.
22) I have twenty or more years before I need to access my retirement, I can afford to take chances.
23) Cash equivalents are simple too weak and undependable to weather a volatile economy.
24) A 25% loss one year means nothing if it is followed by a 45% gain the following year.
25) I believe I can learn how to manage my own portfolio as well as any professional.

Key to the Risk Profile:

Once you have answered all of the questions it is time to add up the number of questions you answered "true" to. True answers are an indicator that you are more comfortable with risk taking as opposed to false answers which would indicate you are more prone to be risk averse.

20-25 True Answers: If you had 20 or more true answers to the risk profile, you are the market maverick that seeks to roll the dice and hit it big. Risk to you is as much a game as it is a concept or possible investment reality. You do not mind investments that may fluctuate in their principal value, so long as they produce a significant return over time. Stocks, real estate, partnerships, initial public offerings and anything that looks like a solid idea that might take off are attractive to you. Your personal philosophy probably relates to the Gambler, Romantic or Prima Donna.

15-19 True Answers: If your true answers fall into this mid-range category, you are more likely to be comfortable with a more balanced approach. Risk is manageable to you as long as there are elements to your portfolio that help to counterbalance higher risk vehicles. You may feel uncomfortable with losses in principal to certain investment vehicles, but you are confident you can manage that risk through diversification, research and other solutions to risk. Stocks, partnerships and other potential high flying investment may be part of your portfolio, but they likely will not dominate your portfolio. You are more closely associated with the Wizard, Scientist or Chef in your outlook on all things financial.

11-14 True Answers: If you fall into this category, you are definitely trending toward the conservative. You should be well and thoroughly diversified in your portfolio with a strong preference for more conservative, less volatile investment vehicles. You may tolerate some risk, such as a stock growth and income fund, but you will certainly not bet your whole future on it. You are probably not afraid to fine tune your portfolio to ensure risk is well mitigated. With the ball rolling down the hill into the court of steady and conservative, your game looks more like the Accountant or Mechanic.

 10 or Less True Answers: If you have less than 10 true answers you are unquestionably risk averse. You want to be as cautious as possible and ensure that your portfolio grows steadily with little fluctuation or volatility. If you fall into this category, you must be willing to accept tradeoffs on higher returns for the stability you expect in your portfolio. Your philosophy in certainly conservative, therefore conservative returns must be seen as appropriate. Bonds, fixed income funds and cash equivalents feel secure to you, despite the limited opportunity for high returns. You may even feel uncomfortable having to select a particular investment if you are not clear about the risks. Your philosophy is more in line with the Accountant, Marionette or Farmer. To you, there is nothing wrong with slow and steady.

The moral of this story is very straightforward. Be honest in how you feel about risk and invest accordingly. It is important to note that your outlook on risk is not a fixed commodity. Just as your opinions on money, politics or religion might mature and progress throughout your working years, so might your outlook on the whole idea of "acceptable risk." It is advisable to re-assess your risk tolerance at least every five years or so and adjust your personal investment philosophies accordingly. Who knows what ideas or new investment horizons will open up to you if you are responsible, consistent and thorough in evaluating your own investment future.

The Giant Investment Product Universe

To begin a journey of discovery all you need to do is pick up a copy of the Wall Street Journal and turn to the stocks and mutual funds section to have laid before you a plethora of investment opportunities. Almost any entity that does business in or with companies in the United States seeks investor capital. Outside of the mainstream investment world there are even greater numbers of self-directed investment opportunities. Every type of investment bears a certain risk. Every type of investment offers a projected return. Every investment has the potential to exceed the promised returns; every investment has the potential to fail in providing desired returns.

Fortunately for most types of investments there is plenty of information defining the specific history of that investment. All mainstream investments have a document that must be provided to the interested investor known as a Prospectus. By law a Prospectus must discuss specific areas of history and risks associated with investing in a particular investment vehicle. A Prospectus contains quite a bit of information and takes time to read and digest. But if it is your money at stake, would not such information be worth your while to study if you are serious about your plan and strategies? In addition, there are web-based information sites and industry periodicals that discuss investment performance, history and future expectations in detail. If you are dedicated to the task, you can compile thorough and adequate information on almost any common investment. Self-directed investments are a different story and require a higher level of expertise, as will be discussed below.

Regardless of the investment types you explore, take the time to become familiar with the history of any stock or investment fund. Sometimes the more subjective issues besides numbers have a story to tell also. Take time to study not only the history of the investment vehicle but the people behind them as well. If you are looking at a particular stock or bond of a company, what has the history of leadership and management been in that company? Is there a lot of turnover at the top? Perhaps the company had stability for a time but unrest at present? How is that company positioned in its industry? Are they a leader? Is the consensus of other experts on finance that the company is on the rise, stable or on the decline? How about the manager of a mutual fund? How many years have they been on the job? What sort of track record have they accumulated? Were there any past funds they managed that prospered or had trouble? There is always a people side to investing. Ask yourself the question:" Would I trust these people or this institution with my money, my friend's money or my family's money?" If you have the right questions to ask, you will almost always find enough information to formulate the answers you need.

Do not discount the professional resources available to you also. Professional brokers, lawyers, investment firms and corporate Human Resource Departments and Benefits Specialists may all be sources of valuable information. Always keep in mind that their agenda is to be helpful, but their plan may not always be your plan. It is up to you to accumulate, process and act upon information that is useful to successfully executing you personal investment plan and strategies. You can also turn to the many industry publications, television programs and internet resources available to provide information and insight into investment vehicles, strategies and current market conditions.

Claims are Claims, and Nothing More

As you undertake research on various investment options, strategies and specific vehicles, keep in mind that almost everyone has something to sell. Experience can be put into hard numbers, but it can also be dressed up and made to look as positive as possible. All legitimate claims made in the investment world are based upon what has already taken place. It really is true that past performance is no guarantee of future results. But past performance is the best indicator you might have of what trends and specific options might remain dependable in the future. Funds and fund managers that have shown a propensity for success in the past have a very good chance of experiencing success in the future as long as they stay on top of their game. But if everyone in the investment world were to be strictly honest, they really cannot completely and accurately predict the future. Any claims that insinuate otherwise are not to be trusted. The investment world is a room full of shifting doors. Opportunities come and go. But you still should not discount the fact that investment vehicles that have a strong track record of success are more likely to maintain that good record. A strong track record of past performance is a general indicator of good research and management and you must assume that most funds will continue that positive operational trend.

But keep in mind that we all live in a world of investment assumptions. Even the highest level and most successful financial managers have to make numerous assumptions upon which they will base their future success. No one get is right every time. Being in touch with your own personal philosophy and feelings regarding risk will go a long way to keeping the claims and enticements of the investment universe in proper perspective. The more informed you are both about the types and histories of products available and how those products fit within your own plan and philosophy, the more you will be able to cut through the noise and clamor of marketing claims and advertising enticements to make informed and appropriate decisions for your own portfolio.

Exploring Self-Directed Investment Alternatives

One of the burgeoning trends in the modern investing universe is the trend towards self-direction of investments. Self-directed investments are defined as vehicles that are not contained in a typical stock, bond or fixed income portfolio and are identified and acquired outside of typical fund management parameters. They consist primarily of such non-traditional paths as partnerships, limited liability companies, real estate trusts and individualized and customized real estate investments. An additional layer of expertise is recommended in entering the self-directed investment world. In the case of many seasoned or entrepreneurial business professionals, self-direction is desirable for at least a portion of their portfolio due to the potential for much higher returns on their investments. As usual, there are additional layers of risk that need to be navigated to arrive at such desirable returns. Self-direction involves investing in real business opportunities that you identify independently. They could be individual stocks or bonds from an established entity, but are more typically entrepreneurial activities such as initial public offerings, start-up partnerships or independent real estate projects that allow you to tax shelter part or all of your returns. There are numerous ways and means you can self-direct your investments if you are in touch with such ground level entrepreneurial endeavors and develop the expertise to profit from them.

A significant portion of self-directed investments deal with either partnership or real estate projects. Partnerships, in the form of Partnerships, Subchapter S corporations or Limited Liability Companies are formed to execute a specific business purpose and define ownership and insulate the participants from liabilities of the enterprise. For example, a group might have a source that has manufactured a new type of dental implant. Doing market research, they determine there exists a global market for such a product. The group forms a Limited Liability Company using their IRAs as members of the company. The funds deposited into the company are used to set up the manufacture, marketing and distribution of the product as well as hire initial employees to run the operation. After five years, the partners, represented by their individual IRAs, have grown the company and sell it to another national corporation and realize a 1500% return on their investment, all of which is tax deferred or tax free depending on the specific vehicle that invested.

Another example would be a group that forms a company with their retirement finds to purchase land, build and rent out an apartment complex. The rental profits would be used as the return on investment associated with the capital necessary to build the complex. The partners hire a real estate management firm to manage the complex and service renters. The partners realize a 25% per year return based on the rental market and rental rates after maintenance and management fees. In ten years the partners sell the apartment complex for a profit of 300% over their construction costs. The total ten year return would be distributed among the partners totaling 450% based on their initial investment.

In each of the above scenarios an opportunity was undertaken. But requisite with the opportunity are additional risks. Knowledge of real estate, rental markets, dental implants, marketing and other business principles is advisable before undertaking any such investment. In each case the partners would either have such expertise or be able to hire such expertise at an acceptable rate. In addition, time is necessary in nurturing a self-directed investment. The balance to that time is a direct understanding of the performance of the investment, since self-directed investors are often functioning on the ground floor of their investment choices. Along with additional risk comes the additional opportunity for control and monitoring of investment performance. There are several professional companies nationwide that can provide further insight into the processes, risks and rewards of self-directed investments. Self-directed companies generally are associated with IRAs or other personally owned retirement plans. In the corporate world of 401K and 457 plans, self-directed options are rare if they are found at all. For anyone with a risk profile of 15 or above, self-directed investments are a world you should at least gain an understanding of. You never know when you might discover the right opportunity.

Adjusting Expectations with Reality

Whatever your risk profile and however your plan and strategies are structured it is important to take a periodic reality check. Investment returns above and beyond the norm are not usual and frequent occurrences. They are often highly specialized and risky undertakings that often require a particular expertise or the fortune of the right contacts to acquire. Take a close look at your portfolio. What are the expectations of performance? What are your personal expectations? Would a panel of three investment professionals share your expectations, or would they be different based on the investments you have chosen? Do you understand the expected realistic returns based on your investment selections? If you do, your reality should approximate your expectations. If you have overblown expectations, you will likely be disappointed and rush to make decisions that are not consistent with your risk tolerances.

Remember that investing for retirement is a marathon, not a sprint. Review your expectations and portfolio in terms of months and years, even decades to maintain a proper and balanced perspective. Do not make adjustments to your plan or portfolio based on false expectations. Be realistic. Underperformance in one year is not the end of the world. Consistent underperformance should have you reviewing your plan and strategies to look for realistic and rational explanations. If your portfolio exceeds your expectations count that as your good fortune and move forward keeping your eye on your long term plan.

In conclusion, you must undertake a personal and professional journey to determine how you feel about risk and be prepared to live within the personal philosophies and guidelines you establish based on the discoveries of that journey. If you can tolerate the volatility that risk brings, structure your plan more aggressively to accommodate those risks. Be prepared to live with the volatility that taking risk brings, but find satisfaction in experiencing the stronger returns whenever they are realized. If you are more risk averse, structure your plan with more balance towards stable returns and less volatility. Take comfort in the fact that your plan will offer slow, stable growth, but do not expect double digit investment returns each year. Do not let disappointments in lesser returns outweigh your distaste for risk. Set your plan and philosophies realistically within the framework of your own honest tolerances and live with the results. There is no better way to be consistent in achieving the success you ultimately envision. Let your preference for risk help to define your vision of success. Not only will you be more consistent in the long run, you will likely be happier as well.

Rule 7 – Determine Your Phase of Life and Structure Your Portfolio Accordingly

As previously discussed, time horizons have an impact on how you might perceive risk and what you consider a priority. Time may heal losses experienced in the short-term with rebounded gains in the long-term. Equally important are the goals that should be attached to and made part of your plan based on the phase of life that you are in. In other words, your retirement plan should and most likely will change and develop as you grow through various periods in your financial and working life. Different phases of life will highlight different emphasis on your plan suggested by the amount of time you have to execute that plan.

The moral of the story is this: as you progress through the main phases of life, your investment priorities and perceptions are likely to change. You should be aware of where you are in the timeline of your plan and make the periodic adjustments that you feel are necessary based on that timeline. Think, for a moment, of attitudes that you or people you know have throughout various periods of life. Young people in their teens and twenties tend to be much more open, free-flowing and carefree when compared to people in their forties and fifties. If you can see a trend towards more measured and conservative attitudes in other areas of life as you age, why would attitudes towards finance and investing be any different? You are much more likely to be aggressive and takes risks earlier in your life phases than you will later. And in the sense of time and risk this is actually not a counterproductive way to think or act. Additionally, you are much more likely to make more informed and educated investment decisions after twenty or thirty years of work experience than you would at the beginning of your career. Understanding the main life phases and how perceptions and attitudes change as well as how strategies and plans might successfully evolve is a dynamic you must become comfortable with.

Most experts and strategists will agree upon four main life phases. First on the timeline are the early years, from roughly age 21 to age 35. Mid-life extends from age 35 to age 55. Pre-retirement runs from age 55 to age 65 and retirement generally is considered after age 65. We will examine the primary considerations of each of these life phases and discuss what should be of primary importance in each phase.

The Early Years – Ages 21 to 35:

As stated earlier in Rule 2, this early stage of working life is the most crucial to begin planning and saving for retirement. Conversely, it is a time in life when few individuals actually think ahead to the importance this phase of life contains. Starting earlier is always better than starting later. The earlier on in life you begin, the more you will have at the end of the game. The main emphasis of the early years, other than getting started as soon as possible, is a focus on *asset building*. Greater risks and higher returns are typical of this life phase since the investment horizon is the longest it will ever be in your working life. Aggressive investment strategies and higher risk and return vehicles are not uncommon in the portfolios of this age group. Obviously the aggressiveness of investing in this phase should take into consideration the individual tolerance of risk, but for most people in this phase, it is full speed ahead. Further, without the burdens of expenses that might be realized later in life, children, college, expanded lifestyles and so forth, this is a time where a significant percentage of income should be dedicated to building an investment base to realize aggressive returns. The more put aside in the early years, the more will be working and earning interest in the later years. The problems with getting started and taking advantage of the early years may not lie so much in the ability to start saving and planning, but in the perception and desire based on the necessity to start as soon as possible. It may seem burdensome to be disciplined enough to set aside a percentage of an entry level income, even though that is exactly what needs to happen.

Retirement planning and investing should appear on the radar of everyone in their early years, even though the tendency is to put off such thoughts. The sooner you begin the better off you will be at the end of your life cycle. This phase is a time in life when you are exploring your career options and may change your course a time or two as you search out the best fit for your skills and ambitions. It takes real perspective and discipline to include early phase retirement planning into the potentially fluid and flexible career path you may experience in this phase. Your approach to your plan and philosophy should also be flexible. If there was ever a time in your working years where higher risk is more tolerable, this is the time. High growth of the assets you are able to put away is the order of the day. The chart below shows a suggested investment mix for the early years:

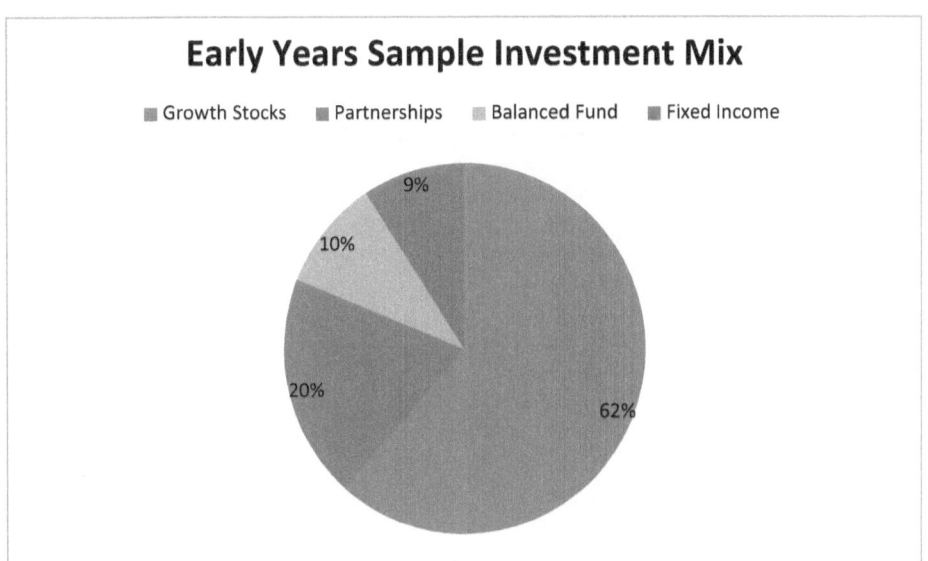

Mid-Life – Ages 35 to 55:

This period of life is defined as the years of steadiness, balancing the *growth* of your assets with the ability of your assets to provide consistent *income* (i.e. dividends, interest and other investment returns) and progressive *asset preservation* into your portfolio. This phase of life also encompasses the most productive years in a typical working career; years where business acumen and career paths are being built and defined. These are years where career experience and career power are maximized, as well as earnings potential. The mid-life period will often be the definitive period of your working life. Whether you have begun planning in your early years or not, these are the years in your working life where you should take greatest advantage of the resources that are available to you. Your planning should continue to reflect lengthy time horizons and should reflect the philosophy of aggression versus risk as you perceive these parameters both conflicting and harmonizing over time.

Most people working in this phase of life have the ability to be flexible with their planning. They are able to add to, broaden and develop their plans and portfolios. Perceptions of risk will likely mature and develop just as your understanding of the working world around you matures. Your plan may be more aggressive in the earliest portions of this phase of life and progressively become more conservative as the years move on. One defining feature of this phase is the growing knowledge and flexibility you have to plan and strategize to any level of risk versus reward you care to entertain. The chart below shows a sample investment mix for the mid-life years:

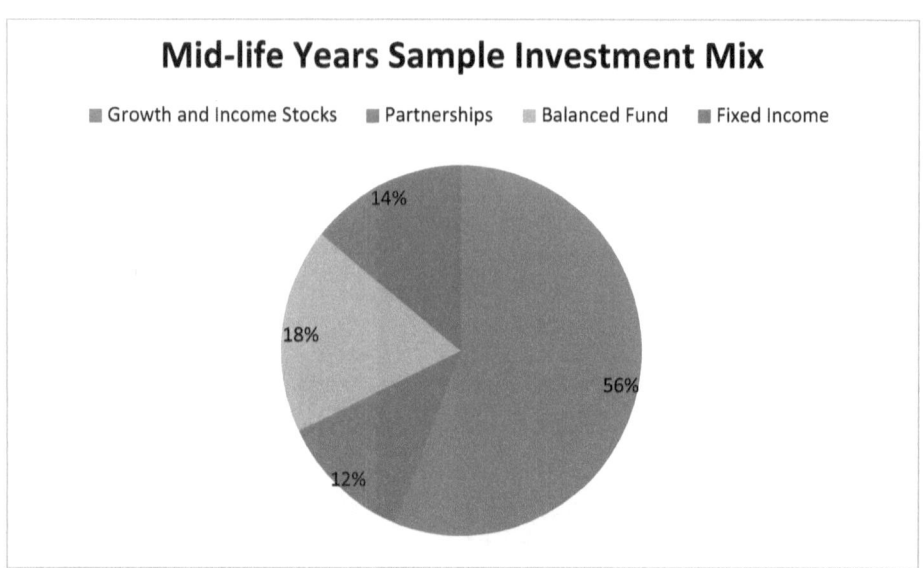

Pre-retirement: Ages 55 to 65:

There are some general and historic assumptions to the ages defined in this phase of life. The age of 65 has been a traditional retirement age in America, with many employers even mandating retirement at that age as a general rule. However, changes in generational saving, the ever-increasing life expectancies associated with modern medicine and general overall health and wellness trends have extended many Americans working lives. Whether it comes from preference or necessity, we are simply living longer and often working longer. Depending on your situation, now or in the future, pre-retirement years may extend longer than this standard, historical period depending on your actual retirement age. The main focus of a plan or strategy in this phase of life should take a shift from income and asset building to *asset preservation*. The overriding philosophy is that at some point at the end of this phase, you are going to begin depending on the assets you have accumulated to begin providing for lifestyle expenses as opposed to recurring earnings through employment.

Your plan and philosophy should unquestionably begin to become more conservative at this point in time. High flying, risky investment that may experience high levels of volatility should begin to be replaced by more stable vehicles. The worst case scenario in this phase of life is to have substantial assets placed in a vehicle that experiences a loss of capital at a time close to retirement, not allowing a sufficient time horizon to recover those losses from future appreciation. A rational philosophy at this point in your investment timeline is to have a portion of your portfolio in volatile investments equal to the amounts you are willing to lose if necessary to achieve potential higher returns. The market downturns of 2007-2009 were devastating to those investors on the brink of retirement who held what they perceived as conservative stock investments that may have lost 40% or more of their value. Many of these investments have returned, while many have not. As you progress through this phase, vehicles that will be most stable in preserving the capital you have accumulated are recommended most. The chart below shows sample investment mix for pre-retirement years:

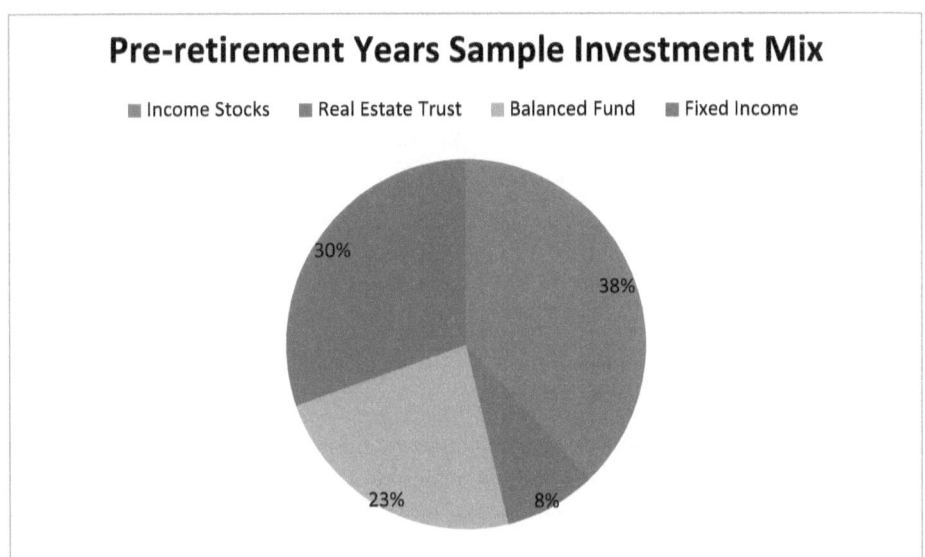

Retirement – Age 65 and Over:

This is the phase of life in which you hope your philosophies and strategies spanning your entire previous working career have paid off. The standard for retirement has historically been age 65. Your actual plan may identify a target earlier or later than this age. That target may need to be a bit flexible depending on past investment experience and planning and the economic environment surrounding the years in which you hope to retire. Nonetheless, at some point in your life, working income will decrease or cease altogether. The time will come when you will need to draw upon the assets that you have accumulated over a working career. However, even though you may not contribute to your retirement fund after your working years are complete, you still need a solid plan to coordinate the amount of *income* your retirement funds produce that you can draw upon while still *preserving capital*. This can often be a delicate balancing act, particularly in an environment, such as the present, where fixed income investments provide very low returns. This is generally a time where you want to minimize risk, but try to provide an investment revenue stream that does not rapidly deplete the principal of you savings. This is the point in life that the magic number you have envisioned and planned for throughout your working life needs to become a reality. The chart below shows a sample mix of investments that might be more appropriate to the retirement years:

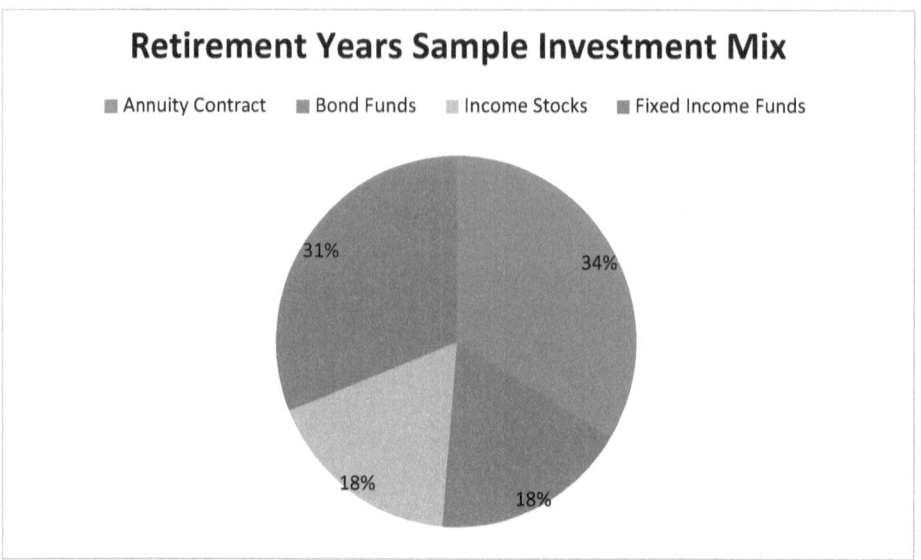

There are a number of strategies, such as annuity contracts or trusts, to provide an income stream from your savings capital upon retirement. The best way to ensure you have hit your target, and thus have the assets necessary to provide adequate income flow, is to pay attention during the previous phases of life and stick closely to your plan. If you have planned correctly, you will inevitably arrive at this point in life in good shape, at least somewhere in the vicinity of your magic number. If you have not planned adequately, you will either be required to continue to work, find an additional source of revenue or you will go through your savings before you have run out of time to enjoy your nest egg.

The main point here is that planning does not stop once you have retired. You have to plan on how to spend your retirement income and how to ensure you have enough income to keep on spending as long as you continue to live. Many other financial issues need to be factored into the equation such as health care, long term care, estate planning and so forth during these years. These subjects are beyond the scope of this discussion, but be aware that part of your plan should include the concepts needed to care for every aspects of your life, recreation, health, housing, daily necessities and the inevitable transfer of whatever assets remain upon your passing. As always, there is a substantial professional infrastructure in place to assist you during these important years.

The Strategies and Benefits of Time Horizons

In each life phase, time plays a significant role in your plan. Early on, the sooner you begin to plan and save, the longer you will have to accumulate assets towards retirement. You can be aggressive in both accumulation and investment strategies with multiple decades of investment time ahead. During mid-life phases you can continue to escalate your savings and planning and still continue to be aggressive with your investment, assuming you have adequate risk tolerance to do so. As you approach the retirement years and your time horizons begin to shorten, so does the opportunity to be aggressive and have time to heal losses that may come from volatile investment vehicles.

Whatever phase of life you are in, be aware of the benefits of time. Plan according to the horizons you identify as relevant. Break down your plan and strategies into sub-plans and strategies based on the time windows available. Most professionals recommend re-visiting your plan at least every five years. Such convenient time frames allow adequate room to consider the influence remaining time horizons may have on your strategies and risk tolerances. Remember, time is always on your side, as long as there is plenty of time to work with. If it is true that on a debt interest never sleeps, neither does a good return on an investment. The longer your money has to work for you, the more work it will do.

The Continuous Tension between Asset growth and Principal Preservation

The greatest challenge to any investment plan or strategy is the ability to grow your savings through healthy returns while keeping your investment principal stable and growing at the same time. Historically, the most prolific earning investments are those investments that carry risk of loss on the principal. The balancing act you will need to achieve in your plan is to realize the highest returns possible while trying to preserve the balance of your savings. This becomes more critical the closer to actual retirement you come. On this subject in particular, seek professional advice. There are many tools that you may utilize, both personally and through professionals, that will allow you to study the history of a particular investment. Whether it is a stock, mutual fund, or other investment vehicle that has the potential for volatility and loss of principal you should be able to locate enough information about the investment to be well enough informed to decide if it fits within your personal philosophy and tolerance for risk. The balance of preservation of principal versus return must always be measured in terms of your personal risk tolerance. It also has to reflect the realistic expectations that apply to most risk versus return scenarios.

Historically it has been possible to realize acceptable returns without too much risk to principal volatility. Diversification is a significant key to attaining this balance. Spreading your investments across a wider selection of vehicles is often the best single strategy to finding the delicate balance between asset preservation and aggressive returns. The exact formula or recipe for this balance will vary from individual to individual, from portfolio to portfolio. Finding this type of balance is as much an art as it is a science. In order to determine if you are comfortable with the balance of your investments, set personal goals or expectations for your investments in terms of both annual returns and degree of volatility. Communicate with other professionals involved in you plan, such as investment counselors of benefit plan administrators, your specific goals. Compare recommendations with past historic returns. Determine of the number add up for you. Fine tune you plan from time to time with these goals in mind.

Crossing the Finish Line - Making a Road Map for the Golden Years

Eventually the day will come when the work clothes will find their way to the back of your closet. Retirement itself is an interesting concept. Is there a time in life when we are truly and completely retired? Probably not. But there is a time when we will all undoubtedly want to shift our focus from being beholden to a schedule required to earn a living to a schedule that revolves around anything and everything else we make plans to do with the remaining years of our lives. The richness of the experience you have following a lifetime of career exertion depends largely on how well you planned and saved throughout those years. You may not even have an understanding at this point in your life and career as to what adventures those years will entail. But be assured, you will find room in your imagination to plan and visualize a number of activities, ideas, people and places that you will want to experience. The term golden years does not refer to your age as much as the opportunities you may create if you have planned well.

One of the most common trends in retirement is the relationship between envisioning and planning and the level of enjoyment each individual has. The more active and involved people seem to be, the more they seem to enjoy and benefit from the retirement years. Conversely, the more active a person is the more they seem to find ways to bless and enrich the lives of others around them. Some activities require little financial assistance, such as spending time with extended family or giving voluntary service within your community. Other activities do take money, such as travel, charitable contributions and supporting the activities of subsequent generations. For this part of retirement you need two distinct things.

The first thing you need is a savings level somewhere in the general vicinity of the magic number you have hopefully been nurturing over the years of planning and saving. The second is a plan to allow the assets you have accumulated to extend over and beyond the course of years you envision spending in actual retirement. That plan should encompass three separate factors. The first factor involves an investment mix that will yield adequate investment income while requiring minimal erosion of your savings from year to year. The second part of that plan includes identifying and budgeting for recurring, discretionary and unforeseen expenses that you may incur year to year. The third factor is proper estate planning through long-term care, life and health insurance, death benefits and wills and trusts. Each of these areas should be undertaken with care and with the assistance of professional advice. The financial industry is rife with experts on maintaining wealth and estate planning. Every retiree should have a circle of trusted professionals that include at least a doctor, an attorney, an investment advisor and an estate planner or fiduciary. You should at least have a workable will and set up trusts as necessary as part of your planning. These functions may overlap within you circle of trusted advisors. It never hurts to obtain more than one opinion on such important, and often delicate and personal, financial matters.

With the issues at least identified, quantified and put into place, you should have a strong foundation from which to enjoy your retirement years with relative ease. And an easier, worry-free retirement is one of the rewards that makes decades of hard work all the more worthwhile. With the right principles, the right discipline, good professional advice and a desire and diligence, you can get there. You CAN be ready and have positive experiences throughout your retirement years, freed from the worry that lack of planning would surely bring. With the right planning, the only questions you will have any significant concern over are how to best spend the time you will have to enjoy the best years ahead. Here's hoping all of your golden years are indeed that...golden!

Afterword

The rules outlined throughout this book reflect the simple but powerful principles necessary to take control of your financial security throughout your working life. No one deserves to have something to show for years of hard work more than you do. And conversely, no one is more responsible for ensuring that you have something to show for all that work than you have. Markets may rise and fall, specific companies and their securities may wax and wane, creative business ideas may come and go, but in the final analysis the buck starts and stops with you. Once you have internalized the basic principles found in each of these rules, it is simply up to you to move forward and start executing the details.

We are fortunate to live in an era where there are numerous allowances within the tax code to make investing for retirement not just advisable, but an absolute necessity. You are missing opportunities if you do not take full advantage of the many vehicles that are ever available to you. While the discipline of investing for retirement requires time and effort, inevitably the rewards will speak for themselves. The investment industry is massive, and continually thriving. Within this industry are those well-trained individuals that can serve as a resource for you. The internet and industry publications are full of information that you can use to formulate an effective and successful plan to get you where you want and need to go. And that destination is a magic number of dollars that you can, will and must accumulate for yourself to enjoy life beyond your working years.

With life expectancies continually on the rise, the golden years can truly be golden for any and all Americans that prepare themselves to harvest the fruit these years can afford. Advances in nutrition, health care, disease prevention and treatment and other areas make life after age 65 not only feasible, but eminently enjoyable. The dynamics of increased life spans and better health and more activity during these years also has financial implications. You will want to have the funds to enjoy this time of life as much as possible. After all, it is during this time you harvest the dreams you have built through decades of a working career. With proper planning, discipline and an understanding of the principles espoused in the rules of this book, you can make. Anyone can make it if they begin early enough and remain consistent throughout their working lives. The principles in this book will greatly assist you in getting to the goals you inevitably must establish and the plans and strategies you must execute. You simply need to get moving and do it. After all, your future depends upon it. Here's hoping you realize all of your best plans and dreams!

www.ingramcontent.com/pod-product-compliance
Lightning Source LLC
Chambersburg PA
CBHW030956240526
45463CB00017B/2734